GREAT PERSONAL IMPACT IDEAS

Dr Peter Shaw

Marshall Cavendish
Business

Dedicated to the staff at

Moorfields Eye Hospital in London

for the superb work they do enabling people

to retain their eyesight.

TITLES IN THE 100 **GREAT IDEAS** SERIES

100 Great Branding Ideas by Sarah McCartney
100 Great Business Ideas by Jeremy Kourdi
100 Great Copywriting Ideas by Andy Maslen
100 Great Cost-cutting Ideas by Anne Hawkins
100 Great Innovation Ideas by Howard Wright
100 Great Leadership Ideas by Jonathan Gifford
100 Great Marketing Ideas by Jim Blythe
100 Great PR Ideas by Jim Blythe
100 Great Presentation Ideas by Patrick Forsyth
100 Great Sales Ideas by Patrick Forsyth
100 Great Time Management Ideas by Patrick Forsyth

FORTHCOMING TITLES:

100 Great Coaching Ideas by Dr Peter Shaw

CONTENTS

Section C: Do

Section D: Don't

Section E: Demonstrate

Section I: Create

Section J: Know

ACKNOWLEDGEMENTS

AT THE END of July 2012 during a busy day of coaching individuals, I was gradually losing the sight in my right eye. A visit later in the evening to the Accident and Emergency Department at the Moorfields Eye Hospital in London led to the diagnosis that I had a detached retina. After an emergency operation the following day I was told to sit still and not move my head for a fortnight.

I was already in discussion with Marshall Cavendish about the possibility of writing this book. Sitting still for ten days provided me with a golden opportunity to write it. The publishers readily agreed.

As I gradually recovered it was a joy to have a very good reason to sit still for ten days, keep my head still and talk into a dictation machine. Writing a book in such a concentrated fashion had the great advantage of enabling me to remember what I wrote in chapter 3 when I came to chapter 93.

I am grateful to the staff at the Moorfields Eye Hospital for ensuring my recovery and for Marshall Cavendish for agreeing that I write this book which provided the best possible recovery therapy. I am dedicating this book to the superb staff at Moorfields Eye Hospital.

I am grateful to Chris Newson who originally suggested that I write this book in the "100 Great Ideas" series. I am grateful to Melvin Neo who has been a helpful and thoughtful editor. Stephanie Yeo has done admirable editorial work on the text. Jackie Tookey typed the manuscript with skill. She understands what I say even when I don't. Helen Burtenshaw has helped to organise the material in the margins of busy days working with me as my Executive Assistant. Their patience and good humour has been very valuable.

I am particularly grateful to Ali McPhail, who has always been such an encouragement to me in working up ideas for workshops. She keeps encouraging me to develop ideas and material to stimulate managers and leaders to 'raise their game'.

I am delighted that Sunil Patel has written the foreword. He and I first began to work together 9 years ago. Sunil always brings a calm thoughtful approach, and delivers. His personal impact comes through his focus and his understanding of people and situations.

I am grateful to colleagues at Praesta Partners who have encouraged me to keep writing and always provide valuable ideas and suggestions.

When I was recovering from the detached retina operation and writing this book, Frances, my wife, was an important source of encouragement; with lots of teasing about the target number of chapters I had set myself to write each day.

Over the last eight years I have worked with a wide range of individuals, teams and groups. Their different situations and varying experiences always provide stimulus for fresh thinking. I am grateful to all of them for the joy of working with them. I hope that in some small way I might have made a contribution to their development as leaders.

FOREWORD

Developing your personal impact is an essential part of effective leadership. This book will be an excellent basis for understanding and developing your next steps.

Personal impact comes from being authentic to yourself and your values. Different people will have varying reactions to you and your approach. Understanding how you come across is an important starting point. You need to be confident in yourself and the type of impact you have. Success comes through being flexible and modifying the approach depending on the context and the people. It is not about applying a rigid formula or set of rules.

Growing your personal impact is a lifelong journey. Widening your repertoire by observing others and trying different approaches will ensure there is freshness in your approach.

The great strength of the book is the way it allows you to weave together different approaches. Your influence comes from using several of them together in one dialogue. The resulting tapestry builds a richness of relationship and impact.

Personal impact is often about enabling, facilitating and inspiring others rather than doing things yourself. What matters is often not what you do, but what did your initial contribution stimulate and what was the ultimate result.

Understanding how impact is affected by cultural perspective is vital in today's diverse economy. Styles and values will be different. No single formula will work. You need to be mindful of the codes and courtesies. What is appropriate deference, and what is too much deference? Peter and I have often reflected on the respective insights of his Christian perspective and my Hindu background.

Impact rarely comes through 'hogging the limelight'. Most people today are cynical about 'grandstanding' and titles. The little things matter. Remember names. Find a personal point of reference and connection. An emotional connection is as important, if not more important, than a logical rationale. Watch the negative impact of ill-thought-through throwaway lines and abrupt comments.

This book provides an accessible store of ideas which are rooted in reality. It is full of practical prompts relevant to a multitude of situations. There are a wealth of ideas to try out. Observe how others react as you try out the different approaches. Ask trusted others to give you honest feedback. It is worth developing your style and approach so you do not become too predictable and maintain creativity and freshness.

The book can provide an excellent basis for discussion in teams to assess how the impact of the whole team might develop. Or individuals might be invited to work through some sections as part of their ongoing development. I encourage you to adopt the ideas in this book and to see how they can improve your impact.

Peter and I have known each other for 9 years. My approach to succesive leadership roles has been strongly influenced by Peter's books, especially his emphasis on vision, values, value-added and vitality in *The Four Vs of Leadership*. Through his personal coaching and writing, Peter has enabled me to grow significantly in confidence in my abilities and to widen my influencing approaches.

Peter has challenged me about how best to handle demanding situations. Conversations with Peter have always led to a constructive way through. He brings wide experience as a former Director General in the UK Government, a wealth of coaching experience of individuals and groups across five continents and insights which flow from his role as a Business School Professor.

My encouragement to you is to use all the wisdom in this book. It is a gold mine. Be willing to experiment and try new things. Watch others and learn from them. Celebrate what works well and learn from what works less well. Be brave and push the boundaries today as you try new approaches.

Sunil Patel
Lead Partner, Health Industries,
PricewaterhouseCoopers LLP
United Kingdom

INTRODUCTION

I WROTE THIS book during the London Olympics of 2012 when the TV screens and newspapers were full of examples of the personal impact of the athletes. The impact for some resulted from leading from the front, for others it was a result of following and then choosing their moment to exert their authority.

The impact for all the competitors resulted from their preparation and their ability to make decisions in the moment. They had to prepare physically, mentally and emotionally. Their performance was a result of their mental attitude as well as their physical preparedness.

Champion boxers often use the power of their left hook. But their impact comes from their ability to move quickly and be adaptable, as well as their capacity to make decisions in the moment about when to move forwards or backwards and when to attack or defend. Good boxers need to be able to anticipate the moves of their opponent, even before the opponent knows what those moves are.

The personal impact of cyclists in team races results from a combination of their individual skills and their ability to operate in a team. They need to be both an effective individual and a team player to succeed. A champion cyclist needs patience, persistence and perseverance, as well as the ability to force the pace and go it alone. Top cyclists epitomise the importance of physical, mental and emotional preparedness alongside resilience.

Personal impact flows from clarity about who we are, what we stand for, where we place our priorities, when we choose to act, and understanding why we have a tendency to respond in a particular way. Crucial to personal impact is knowing ourselves and our preferences well, knowing how we contribute effectively, and knowing what our end goals are.

Personal impact is about delivering outcomes. However elegant our attempt at personal impact, our impact may have been irrelevant if there is no outcome. A key starting point is the outcome you want to achieve after considering realistically, and boldly, what might be possible.

Personal impact stems from getting the tone and the timing right. The strength of the argument is only one consideration. What matters is that you pitch the tone right so that others believe your arguments and are open to be persuaded by them. It is also about getting the timing right so that your views are expressed at a moment when others are most likely to be receptive. Personal impact is occasionally about forcefulness but more often, it is about focus and the fine-tuning of arguments to fit a particular context. Personal impact often flows from patience and persistence. Adaptability and agility are just as important as deliberate action.

This book invites you to think through the personal impact you want to have, and offers practical pointers and prompts for thought. The 100 ideas are split into ten sections based around an active verb. The sections encourage you to think positively about your approach and attitude and what you intend to achieve. They provide pointers about what you might demonstrate, share, ensure, remember and create. The last section focusses on what you know about yourself and what matters most to you.

Each chapter includes an illustrative, hypothetical example which is a prompt for thought. The examples deliberately cover a wide range of different situations. The book is designed so you can read either a section or chapter at a time, or read through the whole book. One approach is to take a section at a time and read through the ten chapters, and then reflect on how the active verb for that section –

be it build, be, demonstrate or create – applies to you and what ideas from the individual chapters you might take forward.

We are all at different stages of our journey in developing our personal impact. My hope is that this book provides a reservoir of ideas to encourage you to develop your own repertoire of approaches to your personal impact, which can then be adapted to suit many varying contexts.

What matters most is making choices about your mental attitude and the tone you want to set. Those people I have worked with who have had the biggest personal impact have had clarity about what they are aiming for, convictions about the values that are most important to them, and the courage to act when necessary. This is accompanied by an attitude towards others that is courteous and caring. Their personal impact has come from exercising both a toughness and a warmth in relation to both themselves and others.

I encourage you to see personal impact as an enjoyable exploration as you build on your strengths, try different approaches, nurture your adaptability, crystallise your learning and enjoy all the interactions that flow from deploying your personal impact in a wide range of different situations.

I hope you enjoy this book and that the thoughts and ideas it stimulates enable you to widen and deepen the different ways in which you impact upon others.

Dr Peter Shaw
Godalming, Surrey, United Kingdom
peter.shaw@praesta.com

SECTION A
BUILD

BUILD A SHARED PURPOSE

THE MORE YOU can build a shared purpose, the more your impact is multiplied, with the greater likelihood that it is achieved without unnecessary aggravation.

The idea

If one person stacks all the chairs in a hall into one corner it might take an hour. If ten people worked together it might take five minutes. When a number of people work together with a common purpose, their combined effort can get the task done more quickly. But if there is disagreement about which corner the chairs should be stacked in, it might take twenty minutes to put all the chairs in the right corner, which would be proportionately a much longer time.

Building a shared purpose is always worth the effort to try to achieve coherence and a sharing of effort and energy. When a group faces the same direction the energy to complete a task flows because there is no hesitancy about the purpose. There is mutual support and the desire to avoid the embarrassment of letting your colleagues down.

If you can persuade some of your colleagues that you have a shared interest in reaching a particular outcome, that outcome is much more likely to be reached than if you had acted alone. If you feel that you are at odds with your colleagues there is bound to be friction that slows down decision making and drains emotions. Time spent on building a shared purpose is always a wise investment. At the very least it can produce acquiescence, if not full support. Acquiescence is much easier to live with than hesitation or opposition. If your course of action then proves worthwhile, that acquiescence can begin to turn into a measure of support.

Building shared purpose is likely to mean some compromises in order to reach an agreed approach. It is usually worth making some compromises to reach a unified approach, as an influential group of people with a similar viewpoint is likely to have more impact than a single voice.

Joe wanted to persuade the football club to move to a different site. He had a particular location in mind but recognised that the first step was for the club to agree that it should look for a different site and be willing to invest in its purchase. Joe was willing to compromise on his preferred location in order to build a shared agreement that the time was right for the club to move on and to invest the time and energy required to raise the necessary investment. Once there was a shared purpose, the momentum grew and the club relocated within a couple of years, which was much quicker than Joe had ever anticipated.

In practice

- Be clear what you want to see achieved.

- Differentiate between the core purpose around which you can build a shared agreement, and your personal preferences, which are secondary.

- Be willing to compromise in order to ensure that there is a shared purpose.

- Acknowledge the contribution of others so the purpose is genuinely a shared one.

- Recognise that acting jointly is likely to create more momentum than acting individually.

BUILD TRUST

WHERE THERE IS trust, individuals will be able to focus on the impact they want to have without suspicion and second-guessing from others. Trust removes unnecessary friction and allows activities to flow in harmony with each other and not in opposition.

The idea

A well-oiled machine runs smoothly. There is no unnecessary friction between the parts. It is as if each part of the machine is trusting the other parts to do their job well.

Trust includes allowing your colleagues to play their part and believing that they will do it well. Trust with partners is about mutual respect underpinned by either a formal or informal contract that each partner abides by. Trust is about supporting each other and not taking advantage of each other. It is about acknowledging each other's contribution and not demeaning it. Your impact depends on trusting other people as you cannot do everything yourself. You need others to play their part so that together, the combined impact is more than the contribution of any one party. The car engine has power because each component plays its part in generating the mechanical force which drives the wheels forward.

Trust is built up over time and results from working jointly on small activities, with the accumulated trust then being transferred to more significant activities. Trust is always two-way. If you want people to trust you, you have to trust them first. It will never be perfect, but a high level of trust can overcome individual mishaps, provided there is an on-going belief and desire for the trust to work well.

Once trust has been broken or manipulated, it can take a long time to rebuild. If there can be open conversation about the event that led to the break of trust then perhaps it can be rebuilt reasonably quickly. When you feel there is a loss of trust, it is likely that there is an issue that needs tackling quickly and openly.

Hannah worked closely with another auditor. When they did joint audits the process always went smoothly because there was a high level of mutual respect. When they thought there might be a problem they would quickly identify how significant this problem was. Their trust was based on professional respect, the stimulus of working together and their enjoyment of each other's company. Hannah and her colleague invested time in building trust with the firms they were auditing. If there was any sense of a lack of trust they knew that they had to demonstrate that their processes were fair and sound. The fact that Hannah and her colleague trusted each other enabled them to build a good level of trust quickly with client organisations.

In practice

- Be willing to put in hard work to build trust.

- Accept that building trust is a two-way process.

- Allow yourself to stand back and trust others to do their work well.

- Resist the desire to keep checking up on and second-guessing.

- Where trust is a bit wobbly, spend time investing in and rebuilding that trust.

- Recognise that trust takes a long time to build up, but can be eroded quickly.

3

BUILD MUTUAL UNDERSTANDING

MUTUAL UNDERSTANDING INVOLVES an honest recognition of difference in terms of background, perspective and aspirations. It provides the foundation for constructive exploration of future options.

The idea

Each individual is different. We each have a distinctive family and cultural background. We have our own set of educational and life experiences. Our emotional make-up is unique. Our aspirations and preferences will be different. How then do we manage to live in harmony when we are all so radically different?

Our personal impact depends on our understanding why and how people are different and then working with and not against those differences. When we know about someone's family and cultural background, we can deduce a lot about their make-up and likely reactions. When we know an individual's preferences we can build a picture of their character. When we hear about their hopes and aspirations we can understand how their values and energy drive them in particular directions.

If you want to have an impact on an individual or a group the first step is to build understanding about their background, personality and character. What motivates them? What is likely to energise them or bore them? The answers to these questions give us data to decide how best to impact them in a way that is likely to produce a constructive response.

A way to build understanding is to draw out what is most important to individuals, and why through open questioning. Spending time in dialogue with someone can build a picture of who they are, making it easier to work smoothly with them. Sometimes imagining that you are another person's shoes enables you to anticipate their likely reactions in different situations.

Francoise was working with a new international partner from Asia. They both spoke French well, but Francoise recognised that he needed to build mutual understanding with his new colleague. The fact that they spoke the same language was not sufficient to ensure mutual understanding. Francoise and his colleague spent time finding out each other's background, experience, skills and ways of working. They built up a mutual understanding that enabled them to work well together. They were pleased that they had invested the time building mutual understanding rather than just assuming that it would automatic simply because they were able to speak the same language.

In practice

- Be willing to spend time building up mutual understanding.

- Recognise that having a common language or a shared profession does not equate to a shared understanding.

- Accept that building a shared understanding is a two-way process that requires a willingness to reveal details about your own background and preferences.

- Recognise that building mutual understanding significantly enhances the prospect of building joint impact.

BUILD QUALITY RELATIONSHIPS

WHEN QUALITY RELATIONSHIPS have been established, there is a greater likelihood of smooth and successful working arrangements, with desired outcomes more likely to be delivered. With quality relationships, surprises and issues are much more easily dealt with.

The idea

When a working relationship is effective there is mutual trust at both a professional and personal level and an acceptance of responsibility and accountability. There is an ability to challenge each other in a way that is constructive. In good quality working relationships there is both a warmth and a desire to be honest about issues, addressing them and finding solutions.

Quality relationships are not just about having fun together. They are underpinned by a shared agenda or intent. The client and the contractor have different objectives. The client wants to buy a quality service and the contractor wants to provide services that clients want to buy. Success for both parties depends on building a quality relationship where there is clarity of intent, a mutual understanding about how the service is to be provided, a respect for both parties and a desire to make the working relationship effective.

Good quality relationships always underpin successful joint ventures. Those relationships are not between two robots but between human beings. Hence quality relationships need to take account of both the rational and the emotional aspects of our personalities.

Once a good relationship has been established, surprises and issues are less likely to occur. Minor differences can be readily sorted out and more significant issues are less likely to be disruptive. In a good personal relationship there is a willingness to talk about what has been learnt from previous experiences, be they good or bad. In a quality working relationship that same willingness to be open about what has worked well or less well can enable those working relationships to become even stronger.

As an Operations Manager, Emma was dependent on support from the Finance Department and regarded it as a priority to build a quality relationship with the Finance Director. This did not mean always agreeing with the Finance Director. Emma wanted to build a mutual respect for each other's position and the opportunity to challenge each other in a constructive way. Emma spent time investing in the relationship and worked with the Finance Director on some minor issues first in order to understand how best they might work together in the future. This equipped her well for when more controversial issues needed to be handled. When differences of opinion arose, Emma and the Finance Director were able to work through them constructively because they had built a quality relationship. Emma could now rely on this relationship as part of developing her impact within the organisation.

In practice

- Decide which relationships are important to invest in.

- Be willing to spend time building relationships and understanding the perspective of others.

- Understand that a good quality working relationship includes both support and challenge.

- Keep reviewing how well relationships are working and always seek to improve them.

- Recognise that the stronger the relationship, the more readily it can cope with surprises or issues.

BUILD YOUR INDEPENDENCE

YOUR IMPACT COMES both because you work well with others and because you bring independent clarity of thought and action.

The idea

The outstanding cyclist in the Tour de France is operating both as a member of a team and demonstrating independence of action. The cyclist needs to judge when they work with others using each other's slipstream, and when they ought to go at it alone and sprint ahead. Their success as the cyclist in a road race depends on understanding the other riders and being able to work with them, as well as the confidence to act independently when necessary.

There are moments in a work environment when you have to act alone. The responsibility is clearly on your shoulders and you have accountability to make a key decision; no one else can or should make it for you. You have sought advice from a range of different people, but it is for you to weigh that advice and reach your own judgement.

We may have spent time in an organisation being able to rely on other people to make the final decision. But it will reach a stage where the responsibility is on your shoulders to make decisions and live with those decisions.

Independence is not about acting irresponsibly on a whim. It is about being liberated from earlier presumptions or prejudices. Your independence is about considering all the evidence and reaching the conclusion that you think is right and taking the action that you think is responsible and needed.

Jake recognised that it was his decision about which training organisation to use to develop the skills of his team. He considered all the evidence, having collected views and recognised the differences in people's needs and preferences. He weighed the range of considerations and set aside some prejudices and previous assumptions. He was clear about his preferred outcome but knew that he had to explain his reasons fully to carry people with him, and had to give his full backing to the individual selected to lead the training. He knew there would be some reservations about the final choice, but he understood that it was his decision both about the choice of trainer and his responsibility to explain the reasons.

In practice

- Recognise when you have acted independently to good effect and draw lessons from that experience.

- Be willing to act independently when the responsibility is yours.

- Always seek to balance building a shared purpose and mutual understanding alongside clarity about who is responsible for making particular decisions.

- Be mindful about what attitudes you need to be liberated from in order to act independently with full integrity.

BUILD THE CREDIBILITY OF YOUR CONTRIBUTIONS

CREDIBILITY GROWS WHEN we are seen to bring realism and a wise perspective. It is important not to hesitate too much before contributing when you feel that you have a worthwhile point to make.

The idea

When you have built credibility others want to listen. Credibility flows from the realism and quality of the contributions we make. If you talk too much you begin to bore your listeners. If you make too many points only some of them will be absorbed. If your contribution includes a random list of strong and weaker points you might be treated with a quizzical look.

On the other hand, if you say nothing you are not building your credibility. You may be seen as irrelevant and gradually left out of key conversations, be they verbal or via e-mail or on social networks. Building credibility requires striking a balance between contributing too much or too little. Success comes through contributing in a thoughtful and practical way, taking into account what others have been saying. It is about making clear, influential points without going on for too long.

Credibility depends on careful preparation so we know what we want to say and express it in a coherent and economical way. The preparation needs to suit the purpose. It might mean detailed reading or investigation in advance. It might involve thinking briefly in the course of a meeting about what key points need to be said and how they can be made in an influential way.

Abigail was part of a committee running a community festival. While others were energetically leading the planning, Abigail had a valuable contribution to make as she had prior experience in running festivals. She bided her time and was selective about the points she wanted to make. When Abigail did intervene she was positive, acknowledged the views of others, and was practical and clear in her suggestions. As Abigail became better known her views were sought after, and she became one of the more influential members of the committee. The reasons for this impact were a combination of her understanding of where others were coming from, and the way she used her previous experience to make practical suggestions and ask pertinent questions. Abigail was not overpowering; she relied on the clarity and quality of her comments to have the impact that was needed.

In practice

- Recognise the relevance of your past experience and your expertise.

- Be willing to focus on key points rather than deliver a scattergun of observations.

- Be ready to choose your moment to make your observations and suggestions.

- Be careful that you neither say too much nor too little.

BUILD A TRACK RECORD OF SUCCESS

NOTCHING UP SUCCESSES is good for your self-esteem, confidence and reputation. The more successes you have, the more influential you will become.

The idea

Success breeds success, both in your own eyes and in the eyes of others. If you want to become an effective public speaker it is best to start with small events in front of a sympathetic audience where you can develop your confidence and your techniques. Buoyed by your progress, your confidence will grow and your willingness to adapt your approach will become stronger.

The successful triathlon athlete will start off with a half triathlon and build their confidence before graduating to a full triathlon and possibly even an ironman triathlon. Once you have swum 3.8 kilometres, cycled 180 kilometres and run a marathon once, you either conclude that having achieved an ironman triathlon you do not want to go through the physical agony again, or you might say, having done it once, I know I can do it a second time.

As we evidence our progress, others will begin to take note. They will be observing how we handle bigger and more demanding challenges. As we gradually build our successes, our reputation will grow. Our impact does not come from one event, it results from building a reputation about consistency in overcoming obstacles and producing good outcomes.

Charlie was an executive coach who worked with people when they took on new roles. He helped them build their confidence to do their new job well and develop the approaches that would be helpful in the initial weeks. Charlie worked with a range of people who attributed their success partially to the type of focussed conversations they had had with Charlie. He built a track record of success. His reputation continued to grow and he was sought after by an increasing number of people.

In practice

- Always be willing to try out new approaches in modest settings.

- Recognise what has contributed to your progress and build on it.

- Keep moving into increasingly demanding situations in order to further develop your capabilities.

- Allow others to see examples of your success without being egotistical about them.

- Keep a litany of examples of your successes which you can use in interviews or bring into conversations where your examples can bring helpful insights for others.

8 BUILD JOY

Our impact comes partially through logic and hard work, and partially through the emotional reactions we generate in others. If we can be the creator of joy in others that is one of the biggest contributors to well-being, and to individual and collective success.

The idea

If you enter a room and there is a sense of lightheartedness and joy it is likely that those present will be feeling positive about the work they do and the contribution they are making. If people are joyful in their work, that joy can become infectious as the natural human reaction is to mirror the emotions and demeanour of the people we are with.

For joy to be sustained it has to be rooted in reality. Deep-seated joy is not about hilarity or believing that the people you are working with are mad. Joy that lasts is more deep seated. It includes a sense of purpose and a pleasure in working with others, together with a personal satisfaction that a job is worth doing, as well as a collective sense of camaraderie. A deep sense of joy can cope with setbacks as it has a momentum that keeps you going when things are tough.

Creating a sense of joy in an organisation requires consistent hard work in building trust, mutual understanding and quality relationships. Joy is the product of a disciplined approach to building a sense of shared purpose and a recognition of the contribution of each individual.

The aspiration to build a sense of joy in a team or organisation may seem trite. But if it can be done it helps build a strength of resilience.

Like a good quality hot air balloon, it can cope with the buffeting of the wind and the rain, and still hold its height and move apparently effortlessly across the sky.

Esther inherited a team that was deflated and humourless. Esther wanted to build a sense of joy in the team but knew that it would take a long time. Members of the team had to believe that progress was possible and begin to see it happening. They needed to feel safe to smile and share humour. They needed to both celebrate their successes and recognise where they needed to develop further. Esther encouraged them and made them laugh. She set a light and yet a purposeful tone. Gradually, more of a sense of joy developed within the team which helped ensure that the team delivered the impact it aspired to.

In practice

- See joy as something worth striving for rather than as something irrelevant.

- Be wary if an atmosphere is desperately serious with no touch of humour.

- Be willing to smile and share humorous reflections and do not consider this a waste of time.

- Invite people to talk through what having a sense of joy in the team would mean and how best can you get there.

9 BUILD OPENNESS

WITH A CULTURE of openness, there can be honesty and frankness that ensures issues are dealt with early.

The idea

Building openness is risky. The more you reveal who you are, the more there is the opportunity for people to use that against you. The more open you are about your hopes and fears, the easier it is for other people to either strengthen your hopes or play on your fears. But when there is a genuine and trusting openness your impact is likely to be greater.

When I was Director General for Finance for a UK Government Department, I believed it was right to be as open as possible with the Treasury and with the National Audit Office. Where data was shared and where there was transparency about the issues and potential problems, there was a much greater likelihood of officials working together in a constructive way.

Lack of openness breeds suspicion. We cannot be transparent about everything: negotiating positions have to be prepared in private, but the more open we are and the more that trust is built up, the greater the likelihood that difficult problems can be addressed co-operatively with deliverable resolutions.

Openness is not about giving away all your secrets. It is about coming to conversations with an open mind and being ready to listen. It is about addressing jointly a difficult issue and leaving your prejudices outside. It is about being willing to share your views and not let concerns fester and grow out of proportion.

Henry was concerned that each member of the marketing team was being secretive and addressing their responsibilities in a different way. Henry was certain that if the members of the team were more open with each other they could learn from each other's experience and become less competitive. He persuaded them that sharing their expertise was far more likely to lead to success than being proprietorial about their particular sector. Henry convinced them that the more open and transparent they were, the greater the likelihood of the marketing department's overall success.

In practice

- Be wary when you are very protective of information and expertise that you have.

- See the potential benefits of being more open and transparent while recognising that boundaries of confidentiality are crucial.

- Experiment with being more open and transparent about how you are seeking to tackle issues on your agenda.

- Seek to build a culture of greater openness and draw attention to examples of where this has worked to the advantage of the team as a whole.

10 BUILD YOUR PERSONAL SUPPORT

BUILDING YOUR PERSONAL support is a crucial ingredient to ensuring that you make the best possible personal impact. Skimping on this is false economy.

The idea

What is the personal support you need to ensure you keep your equilibrium and make the best possible impact? An Olympic athlete draws from the support of a professional coach, the encouragement of colleagues, and practical help from those who enable them to keep up the regular discipline of training.

What is the personal support that is most important to you in your work? It is likely to include the encouragement of friends and clarity of direction from your boss. You need IT support that is reliable. You will either manage your own diary efficiently or rely on someone else to manage it for you. Ideally you can also draw on coaching support to help you focus in your work. Every top sportsperson draws on the expertise of a coach. Everyone in a work context would benefit from focussed coaching conversations to reach their full potential.

To be successful we need the personal support of trusted others both in the workplace and outside of it. We need people who can tell us the truth and be honest with us if we are becoming irrational or too preoccupied or too obsessed. The best personal support is both very challenging and unrelentingly supportive.

Eleanor knew that if she was going to be successful in her role and have the impact she wanted, she needed a support team. She was able to enagage a part-time executive assistant who managed her diary. Eleanor also ensured she had good quality IT support. She had the benefit of a mentor with a senior role within the organisation who gave her sound advice.

Eleanor worked with an Executive Coach who enabled her to focus her performance and address any issue where she needed to have an impact. Eleanor had a colleague with whom she had a strong, mutual relationship: they were both committed to each other's success. Two good friends from outside the office always made her laugh when she needed to lighten up. Eleanor had built her group of supporters and knew she could always rely on them.

In practice

- Be clear what is the personal support you need in order to give your best.

- Be relentless in ensuring you have the right mix of personal support .

- Press hard to get the coaching you need, if you think that working with a coach will enable you to significantly improve your impact.

- Be clear about the balance between what only you can do and what others can do as part of your personal support.

- Never take for granted those who provide you with personal support.

- Accept that the most important ingredient in ensuring your personal impact over the longer term is the quality and consistency of your personal support.

11 BE ACCESSIBLE

BEING ACCESSIBLE DOES not mean you are at the beck and call of everyone at any time, but it does mean that when people need to get access to you, they are able to do so. Rationing your accessibility in a reasonable way is important.

The idea

Being accessible does not mean that you are happy to be interrupted at any time by anyone for any reason. Developing a reputation for being accessible is a result of your colleagues knowing that they can be in contact with you when needed.

If a colleague knows that they can talk to you when necessary, it gives them a peace of mind which is likely to mean that they do not need to talk to you very often. But if you have an aura of inaccessibility there is likely to be an underlying concern that you are not as accessible or approachable as you might be and that you may not be available when needed.

Building a reputation for accessibility involves using the full range of communication, including verbal, e-mail, texting and social networks. Texting is an excellent way of communicating short messages and being accessible to briefly answer individual, factual questions.

Rationing your accessibility is inevitable if you are to use it to best effect. It may mean giving people quality time rather than quantity time. Giving people your sole and undivided attention for a short, focussed period can be far more powerful than a long, rambling conversation. You may want to ration your accessibility to particular times of day. Working in an open plan environment requires differentiation between types of accessibility, be it for a short exchange at the desk, or a longer interaction in a more private space.

Your colleagues and boss need to know how to contact you. This does not mean being at their immediate beck and call, but that there will be opportunities for different types of interaction, and that they know the best means of getting a quick reaction from you on something urgent.

To have a personal impact you need to be accessible within a reasonable period when people want to know your views. But you need to control how you ration your time and how you adapt your approach to meet varying needs at different times.

Simon used to get annoyed because his boss was always asking him questions, which meant that he was constantly being interrupted in his work. Simon tackled this by looking at his boss' diary and noting the time periods when he was likely to be tackled by his boss. Simon also discussed with his boss how best they could work together. His boss readily agreed that they should meet for a substantive period once a week, and that they should allocate 15 minutes for catching up each day. They agreed to use texting in emergencies if one of them was not in the office. This new pattern meant that Simon was accessible to his boss in a pre-planned way. Both of them felt the new arrangements were a great improvement.

In practice

- Be clear about who is likely to want you to be accessible.

- Outline arrangements for your accessibility to key people.

- Be willing to use a variety of means of communication to demonstrate your accessibility.

- Be willing to ration your accessibility and focus it.

BE FOCUSSED

Be willing to look at the wider context but always come back to what you want to focus on. Be careful if your focus gets diluted too much.

The idea

The archer is focussed entirely on the target and the runner is focussed on the finishing line. The baseball player is focussed on the ball that is flying towards him. The ability to focus hard in an individual moment is a precious gift.

Success comes because we are able to focus on what matters most at a given moment in time and then switch that focus to an equally important priority shortly thereafter. Focus is not just about a relentless push towards one particular objective. It is about being able to juggle between a number of different objectives, and being single-minded about dealing with each of them in turn.

Our personal impact comes through the confidence others have in us to address a single issue with clarity and verve, combined with the ability to focus successively on a number of different tasks and objectives. This is not about a superhuman attempt to focus on 200 tasks at the same time. It is about being able to be selective and focus on a limited range of tasks which may well be at different stages of gestation.

The maxim that "if you have an urgent task, give it to a busy person" is true to life. If someone is able to focus effectively on a number of different tasks they will often have the capability to focus on an additional urgent one. But the person who is in demand must keep deciding to drop or pass on some of the tasks in order to create room for new requirements.

Megan felt pushed around by different demands upon her. She knew she had to focus on what was most important. She agreed with her boss on the four key priorities for the next month and ensured she focussed on those. She built a reputation for focusing on delivering key outcomes. Because her colleagues knew she got things done they sought focussed conversations with her about their next steps on a range of different projects.

In practice

- Observe others who focus well.

- Be clear about what you need to focus on over the next month in order to have the impact you want.

- Seek to reach an agreement with your boss about what you should focus on.

- Practice the art of focusing on successive individual tasks during the day.

- Be willing to say that some tasks need to be dropped or given away if you are required to focus on new tasks.

13 BE CONSISTENT

CONSISTENCY BUILDS RESPECT and trust. If people know they can rely on your consistency, they will let you get on with things more readily and not try to second guess you.

The idea

A reputation for consistency is an essential part of personal impact. If the work you do is always of a consistent quality your colleagues are much more likely to let you get on with tasks and not second guess you. Your boss is more likely to delegate and leave you to complete your tasks rather than be forever looking over your shoulder.

Consistency does not require doing everything to perfection. If every task you did was perfectly executed it is quite likely that your output would not be as high as it should be. Consistency and fit for purpose go together. Someone whose team produces consistently good results is much more valuable than a team that is brilliant one day and sloppy the next.

Consistency is also about personal demeanour. The individual whose mood is consistent and who is always thoughtful and a good contributor is much more likely to be invited to be part of future conversations. To become influential you need to be involved in key discussions. The person who is known for consistency will be sought after. We may think that people do not want us present because we are not outstandingly creative, but consistent, good, practical, common sense is always going to be valued.

Consistency does not mean being boring or monotone. It is about bringing an evenness of temperament and matching your comments to the needs of a particular context. It is about finding an equilibrium whereby you draw on your experience and wisdom to produce consistently thoughtful contributions which people take seriously and which are, therefore, influential.

Toby knew that what his bosses valued was his consistency in being able to clearly represent the views of buyers. Colleagues always wanted him as part of discussions because they knew that he would not be emotionally disruptive. They knew his thoughtfulness would be invaluable as they talked through how they were going to market particular products to clients. His colleagues knew that they would not get brilliant insights from Toby but they would always get consistently good, practical comments.

In practice

- See being consistent as a valuable and not a boring quality.

- Recognise that others value consistency and do not see it as irrelevant.

- Be clear how you want to put across your measured, thoughtful points in a way that gets others' attention.

- Recognise that your consistent thoughtfulness can complement the more creative ideas of others.

- See consistency in your demeanour as a way of winning friends and influencing people.

14 BE RESPONSIVE

HAVING A REPUTATION for being responsive means that others will seek your view and contribution which will enhance the prospect of your being influential and having a personal impact.

The idea

Being responsive is not about being pushed around by every latest whim. It is not about dropping everything one minute to do something new and then an hour later dropping that new task to take on the latest request. Being too responsive can lead to confusion, chaos and a lack of confidence.

Being responsive is about seeing a need and taking action where appropriate. It might be offering the services of one of your staff, or pointing someone in the right direction or suggesting that a particular internet site is going to be helpful. Being responsive is not about doing everything yourself, it is often about being an effective sign post able to alert others to the best way of getting information or answering their questions.

Being responsive is also about steering a conversation in a way that takes account of the key needs and demands and takes the conversation into a constructive space to enable a way forward to be shaped.

The tennis player is responding to the serve by hitting a strong, directed shot back. When we are asked a tough question the good response is direct and deliberate. Being responsive is not about being random, it is about choosing the way you respond so that your response meets the needs of a situation.

Being responsive is not a sign of weakness. It is a sign of strength to be responsive and adaptable to the changing requirements of a situation. Being responsive sits alongside being consistent in terms of getting the balance right so that your response fits the purpose.

Imogen was learning to work for a new government minister. She wanted to be attentive to the minister's requirements and built her reputation with the minister by being responsive. Once that relationship was established she was able to agree with the minister what should be her priority tasks. Imogen had to demonstrate her responsiveness first before the minister was willing to agree on what would be her top priorities and what would be lower priorities.

In practice

- Recognise when you need to be responsive quickly to others.

- Allow yourself to be responsive when new priorities arise.

- Be careful about being too responsive to too many requests at the same time.

- Do not let your ability to respond well lead to your taking on too much.

- Push back when you need to, to ensure others do not take advantage of your ability to be responsive.

15 BE INTERESTING

Your personal impact is enhanced if people want to hear your views. Always bringing interesting thoughts, facts and ideas to a conversation will make people want to talk to you.

The idea

The person who brings interesting perspectives and ideas is always sought after. If you can keep up-to-date with new information and intelligence you will always have something to contribute that other people will be interested in. The more you talk to clients and customers and different stakeholders, the more you will build up perspectives and be able to share interesting stories and insights. People will want to talk to you because you bring an up-todate perspective.

We enjoy talking to interesting people who have relevant or parallel experience, or a perspective from a different country, or bring the viewpoint of people whose views are not often heard. How can we be interesting to people we want to influence?

Before having any significant meeting it is worth reflecting on what other points of information or insight you can bring that are going to be useful. It is like bringing a gift to somebody as part of a meeting where the gift helps build the emotional bonding. If you are giving someone information that they find interesting or a viewpoint that they find valuable, then emotionally they will be more favourably disposed towards you. This is not about manipulation, it is about treating every conversation as an exchange where if you want something from another person, it is helpful to be bringing a gift for them.

Zoe knew that the chief executive of the local authority was very interested in what was happening in a local community area. Whenever Zoe was scheduled to meet the chief executive, she briefed herself in advance on what was happening in that area and was always able to draw on snippets of news that she knew the chief executive would find of interest. Her reputation for always bringing interesting stories meant that the chief executive was happy to see her on a regular basis, which ensured she had access to the chief executive and the opportunity to influence him. Zoe kept a careful eye on which themes the chief executive was developing an interest in and, at subsequent meetings, brought information and insight about those areas. This approach further enhanced her reputation for responsiveness.

In practice

- Be willing to collect interesting stories and share them.

- Take note of what your boss and colleagues are particularly interested in and be ready to share your latest stories and insights with them.

- Keep up-to-date with pertinent facts, perspectives and trends: be willing to share that information.

- Keep listening to what others are saying: listening is never wasted.

- Communicate interesting information in e-mails and texts as well as verbally.

16 **BE CURIOUS**

IT IS WELL worth to always be curious about what is happening and why. Curiosity will stop us from becoming 'stale' and continually give us new insights.

The idea

It is often said that "curiosity killed the cat". Sometimes curiosity can lead us into areas of danger. The cat that is too curious about the mouse running across the road gets run over by the passing car. The child that is too curious about a piece of garden machinery might get their fingers trapped in it and yell in pain.

Curiosity can sometimes get the better of us and lead us to explore places that are best left untouched. Curiosity can get us into trouble in a work context if we tread too heavily into other people's territory. But curiosity is a fantastic gift. The more curious we are, the more we will want to understand why people behave as they do and why the dynamics of a situation lead in a particular direction.

Every team needs people who are gifted in curiosity. It is their questions and exploration that can help a team view issues in a new way. Questions about "why have we always done it this way", or "what would happen if we did it that way", can be very powerful. Explicitly 'commissioning' someone to be the person who brings curiosity can legitimise asking seemingly irrelevant questions that open up new possibilities.

Someone who is known for a sense of curiosity and exploration is likely to be sought after and thereby become influential. If everyone wanted to spend all their time exploring and being curious, nothing would get done, but every team needs people who have the gift of curiosity. Each of us needs to allow space to develop and exercise our curiosity to keep our minds fresh and insightful.

In practice

- Allow yourself to be curious about why things are as they are.

- See exploring ideas as a strength and not a distraction.

- Celebrate the gift of curiosity in your team and in yourself.

- Set aside time to be curious.

- Be willing to share the results of your explorations of different ideas and possibilities.

- See curiosity as a gift to enjoy and not as a distraction.

BE ENCOURAGING

ENCOURAGEMENT IS ONE of the most worthwhile gifts to give people. We need encouraging to keep up our motivation. To be fully effective, encouragement needs to be linked directly to someone's specific contribution or gift and not be a vague expression of praise.

The idea

We can all look back on those who have encouraged us. We have mental pictures of our parents, our teachers and our friends who were sources of encouragement. I know from my current experience that positive encouragement to my two-year-old grandson brings cheerful results.

We can encourage others through our words and actions. Practical encouragement about a job well done lifts someone's spirits and reinforces what they are doing well – hence the importance of being specific in feedback. The language of "I encourage you to do more of" includes both the acknowledgement of a strength and a steer to use the strengths in a constructive way.

Some people ration their encouragement to see how long people can survive without it. This may be the right approach for some, but most of us thrive better on regular encouragement. Some are hesitant to express a lot of encouragement for fear that it is seen as flattery or trite. Some people may not look responsive when they are encouraged, which could be more about shyness and reserve than not liking complements.

We often think that those in senior roles do not need encouragement. We assume that to get to their positions they must be able to look after themselves. But encouraging comments to those in senior roles are often appreciated just as much. It is likely to be counter-productive to compliment people purely because you want to influence them. Such flattery will be seen through before long. But genuine comments of encouragements to our seniors are part of building a good quality engagement which leads to the influence and impact you want to have.

Sunil enjoyed encouraging others. He delighted in identifying things they had done well and playing this specific encouragement back to them. Increasingly, people asked him for feedback as well as encouragement. The trust he had built up enabled him, as part of his encouragement, to add in brief, practical development points.

In practice

- Don't be apprehensive about encouraging individuals.

- See encouragement as a way of reinforcing what people are doing well.

- Understand when people are likely to be hesitant and need encouragement to be more confident in using their skills and expertise to the best effect.

- Observe how encouragement affects you and be ready to use a similar approach with others.

- Recognise when encouragement might be interpreted as flattery and root your comments in precise examples to help avoid this reaction.

18 BE REALISTIC

THE ABILITY TO bring realism to any situation without getting bogged down by the details is a gift. To be known as rigorously realistic will mean you are sought out and influential.

The idea

Being realistic is about seeing a situation as it is. It is about not being overwhelmed by an emotional reaction. It is about keeping events in perspective and not allowing yourself either to go on a spiral of dejection or blurring realism with unwarranted optimism.

Bringing realism is about being rooted in the facts, being honest about the implications, being clear about what is possible or not possible and being decisive in your actions. Realism involves bringing previous experience to bear, knowing whose views are likely to be accurate and bringing a cool, rational approach that is based on evidence. Realism is about recognising the problems that need to be solved and those that will not solve themselves.

Realism is about finding practical options to move things forward. Negotiations may seem to be stuck, so what are the realistic ways of moving them ahead? A particular negotiation may seem to have reached an impasse: what are the options that need to be explored in order to progress?

Sometimes realism is about saying we must wait; there is nothing we can do until resources are available or attitudes change. In this case realism is not about defeat, it is about acceptance that at this point in time agreement to move forward is not going to happen. Realism includes keeping an eye open about how the context is changing and when what was previously impossible now becomes an option.

When the going gets tough there is a risk of over-optimism or complete dejection. The person who continues to be realistic can help formulate the foundation for progress and thereby become particularly influential.

Barbara felt bombarded by people's scepticism about whether a particular initiative was going to work. Barbara kept repeating that the aspirations were realistic. She said the groundwork had been done and the evidence so far was encouraging. Therefore, it was realistic to believe that the initiative would be successful. Barbara kept rooting her realism in facts: gradually there was a growing acceptance that her realistic approach was valid and reasonable.

In practice

- See the ability to be realistic as a gift.

- Base your realism on the latest facts and evidence.

- Be mindful when people's emotional reactions might begin to blur the realism about what is doable.

- Cross-check your views about what is realistic with others you trust.

- Ensure that the next steps are based on facts and evidence and not instant emotions.

19   BE ENGAGING

To BE ENGAGING is to generate creative discussion and interaction. Engagement involves both heart and mind, and is about engaging with the whole person.

The idea

To engage is to speak with your eyes as well as your mouth, and to be listening with your ears as well as your other senses. To engage is to be mindful of someone's beliefs, views, concerns and expectations.

Sometimes engagement involves intellectual debate. But engagement that influences and has impact is always at more than one level. Engagement with someone you meet for the first time starts with finding a reason for that engagement. If it is purely factual it is likely to be a transactional and rather dull engagement. If the interaction has a sense of warmth and welcome, then it is likely to be more enjoyable. The receptionist who smiles and gives a warm welcome elicits a very different response from the cold and clinical receptionist who is purely focussed on giving us a pass to the building.

We feel at ease with people with whom we have had a good level of engagement in the past. The question is how can we reach a level of engagement quickly with people we know less well. Success comes through allowing ourselves to be relaxed with people, finding the topics about which they are comfortable talking and demonstrating that we are able to discuss subjects that they are interested in.

Effective engagement is about giving people our sole, undivided attention and not boxing them in or closing them down. Engagement involves giving people space to gradually feel at home with you so they are willing to express their views without hesitation.

Louis felt disengaged from two key people in the organisation. He knew he needed to engage with them because there would be forthcoming issues on which he wanted to seek their expertise. Louis decided that he should set aside time to talk to these two individuals informally. He thought about what he could say to them that they would find useful.

Louis gradually built his relationship with these two people and felt the sense of engagement becoming stronger. When he needed their involvement on a particular piece of work they gave him the time and contribution he wanted. Louis was certain it had been worth the time and effort building a stronger sense of engagement with his colleagues. He resolved to keep in touch with both of them on a monthly basis.

In practice

- Who do you engage with most easily and how can you use that same approach with other people?

- Who have you slightly lost touch with and need to rebuild a strong sense of engagement with?

- Who might you now focus on to build a new, stronger engagement with based on shared interests?

- How best do you demonstrate to yourself that time spent on engaging with people is always going to be worthwhile, even if the benefits are longer term?

- What works for you best in terms of reaching a constructive level of engagement with new people quickly?

20 BE FORGIVING

Forgiving other people and yourself is crucial to moving on successfully. Without forgiveness issues can fester and we can lose focus when tackling new issues.

The idea

When someone has failed to deliver should we forgive them? If we have invested a lot of time in them and ensured they have the right experience and expertise, and they still fail to deliver, do we still forgive them?

If we want people to be adventurous and take risks, mistakes will be made. If we want a "no blame" culture then we have to allow people to learn from their mistakes and move on. Perhaps forgiveness is only relevant when individuals or teams recognise that they made mistakes and are clear about how they want to move on and intend to learn from prior errors. In these cases, forgiveness is a natural part of enabling people to have a second go at something.

Unless we forgive others they cannot completely move on. We can have a negative impact on someone's confidence if we keep returning to errors of the past. Similarly, we can help an individual's confidence grow in leaps and bounds if we enable them to work through previous mistakes and learn from them, even when we have felt let down. As we forgive others we strengthen the bond with them as they learn from difficult experiences.

Self forgiveness is equally important. If we feel our impact is not as great as it should have been and do not forgive ourselves, then we will be constantly returning to those memories of disappointment. If we can forgive ourselves when we have been less than fully effective and move on, we can liberate ourselves from those memories of past failure to have more impact in the future.

Ruth felt that she had let down her hockey team because she had failed to stop the ball from going in the net. A fellow defender said to her, "Don't worry, these things happen." That sense of forgiveness lifted Ruth. She knew she had to move on from her mistake and forgive herself. As the game progressed, the last thing she wanted to do was to keep reminding herself of the goal that went in. Her self talk was direct – now was the moment to move on, play wholeheartedly for the team and forget the goal scored by the opposition.

In practice

- Be conscious if you are keeping resentments about others which you need to forgive and forget.

- Be ready to forgive someone who has recently let you down when you know that they have learnt from this experience.

- Be willing to say you forgive someone in order to release them from feeling badly about something that went wrong under their watch.

- Remember to forgive yourself when you have made misjudgements which you now need to move on from.

- On a regular basis, decide who you want to forgive, and what about your own actions you want to forgive.

21 DO PREPARE

FOCUSSED PREPARATION IS always important, but with too much preparation you can become stilted, rigid and ineffectual.

The idea

Good quality preparation is never wasted, but preparation does not start with what you want to say. Preparing yourself is about spending a few moments to understand where others are coming from, being mindful of their concerns and recognising their likely emotional reactions. You are then in a much better position to judge the right content and tone of your contribution.

Judging the appropriate level of preparation is a key decision. If you are to be scrutinised by a panel or an investigating committee you will want to prepare in detail for a range of different questions. If you are giving a speech at an informal gathering, reflecting on a couple of themes you want to use is all the preparation that is needed.

If you are ill-prepared, you can be caught off guard. If you over prepare, you can be too constrained and not adaptable to the mood.

On his journey by train into work Oliver took twenty-five minutes to prepare for three meetings. He knew he had a difficult meeting with the Finance Director about an overspend on a project: he thought carefully about the likely questions and how he could best answer them. He was also going to speak at an off-site meeting for some of his staff: he wrote down a few headings about the points he wanted to make and the stories he wanted to tell. He was giving a farewell speech at a small drinks party. He smiled as he reflected on the theme for that light-hearted speech. He arrived at his destination having done the preparation he needed for the three very different events.

In practice

- Always seek to allow some time, however brief, to prepare for any meeting or engagement in your diary.

- Start with where other people are coming from and what their expectations or needs might be.

- Remember that preparation is as much about tone as it is about content.

- Decide deliberately whether you are going to prepare in detail or just have a few headline points.

- Have some key phrases ready that sum up the points you want to make.

- Beware having a full script if it can make you seem too stilted.

- Be adaptable in deciding on the type of comments you make.

22 DO BE ON TIME

BUILD A HABIT of being on time or early for meetings. This will enable you to be calm and aware of what is happening.

The idea

The individual who arrives late, flustered and dishevelled is likely to have undermined their impact before they utter a word. If we are waiting for someone and they rush up hastily reciting all the reasons why they are late, we smile politely and are perhaps not entirely convinced by their apology. The person who is late but gets away with it is someone who apologises briefly, is calm and collected, and moves straight onto the agenda without bemoaning the inadequacies of the transport system.

Being on time is an expression of courtesy and respect. But it is also about giving yourself the opportunity to quieten, calm down and focus. The ideal is to arrive a few minutes early for important meetings so that there is the opportunity to become centred and focussed. There is a risk of regarding the 'spare' time when you are early for a meeting as wasted time, when this can be valuable, quiet preparation time.

Arriving a few minutes early for a meeting allows you to choose your seat and exchange a few words with other participants. It allows you to gauge other people's moods as they enter the room, which can be invaluable in enabling you to pitch your contribution effectively.

Emily set her watch three minutes early. She always aimed to be on time at meetings according to her watch, which meant she was early. She found this an invaluable technique. When she got to a meeting room she would always breathe more deeply to calm herself, get a glass of water and remind herself to be open, thoughtful and ready to contribute.

In practice

- Plan ahead so you are not late for meetings.

- Know how best you calm yourself and do so in those two or three minutes before the start of a meeting, or conversation.

- Be strict about moving on from one engagement so you are not late for the next one.

- If you are late either apologise briefly or slip in quietly while keeping calm, and ensuring that you pick up the mood quickly and get onto other people's agendas rather than yours.

- Ensure that your day is planned so that the time commitments are doable.

- If you are going to be late let people know in advance.

23 DO USE STORIES

PEOPLE RARELY REMEMBER bullet points but may remember some key facts. Your audience is much more likely to remember stories. A story that catches our attention will bring an emotional as well as a rational response.

The idea

A long, rambling story can be tedious, distracting and appear irrelevant. A short, focussed story can catch our attention, particularly if we can visualise it as well as hear the words.

The individual who can make their message come alive by giving short, clear examples of success is more likely to catch the attention of the audience. If a consultant can tell a story about a successful piece of work in another organisation, their credibility rises. If the interviewee can tell a story about the impact they had in a similar situation in the past they are more likely to be seen as a credible candidate. If the engineer can tell stories about how their skills have led to successful projects in the past, they are much more likely to win respect with others wanting them on their team.

A good story needs a punch-line. The reason for telling a story needs to be clear in your mind while you tell it in a succinct manner so your listeners are open to the message that comes through. A story that is too long will lose people. Keep rehearsing your stories so you refine them down to the key points and can tell them with lightness.

Jack was being interviewed for a director post and understood the skills that were being sought. He prepared a number of examples of how he had used these skills in the past. He practised articulating these stories with a coach and steadily reduced the length of the stories, honing the punch-lines. It was the power and humour of these stories which enabled Jack to appear highly credible for the job he was being interviewed for.

In practice

- Observe who tells stories well, and in particular how they bring out the key point of the story.

- Think through how much context is necessary to enable a story to sound credible.

- Practice using stories as part of the way you communicate in informal contexts and seek feedback about how effectively those stories get your message across.

- When you have a story you want to use in a presentation, practice it and then practice it again at half the original length, and then at a quarter of the original length. This helps hone down any story to key phrases.

- Know what people will visualise as you tell them a story and ensure that you include these visual elements.

- Practice a lightness in the way you tell stories and allow yourself to smile at your own stories.

- Give people a moment to reflect on your story before you move onto your next point.

DO VARY YOUR APPROACH

IF YOU VARY your approach you are more likely to catch the interest of others and be fully engaged yourself. Widening your repertoire so you can respond in different ways means you are less likely to be thrown by the unexpected.

The idea

If someone is predictable we tend to write them off. We tell ourselves that we know what they are going to say and, therefore, we do not really need to listen to them. Most of us have developed approaches that work well in meetings, conversations or presentations. While we may use these techniques to good effect, we can rely too much on one or two tried and tested approaches: they may not always be appropriate.

Others are much more likely to keep listening to us if there is an element of surprise. If we vary our approach this will kindle their curiosity. If we can balance doing what we are good at, alongside widening our repertoire of approaches, we can become ever more equipped for the range of situations we find ourselves in.

Isobel had always relied on being able to put forward persuasive arguments. She assumed that the power of her logic would get the agreement of her colleagues. The risk was that her colleagues felt rather brow-beaten and overwhelmed, with the consequence that their support for her proposals was often lukewarm.

Isobel decided that she needed to talk individually to her colleagues more often prior to a meeting in order to understand where they were coming from. As a result, when she presented proposals in formal meetings there was more support for what she wanted to achieve. Talking to people in advance aided her in achieving the outcomes she wanted, and her impact was better informed because she had heard the views of her colleagues.

In practice

- Be conscious of the approaches to people, meetings, conversations and presentations that work well for you and recognise what you are good at.

- Keep experimenting by adapting your approaches, initially in less important contexts.

- Keep observing others and learning from how they adapt their approach.

- View adapting your approach as a sign of strength and not weakness.

- Celebrate when you have adapted your approach and when it has worked, and add it to your repertoire.

- View bringing an element of surprise as an important part of your repertoire.

25 DO BE PERSISTENT

BEING PERSISTENT IS a strength when you believe you are right, provided you are not "bashing your head against a brick wall".

The idea

The successful explorer will always be persistent. Their determination has carried them through doubt and uncertainty and enabled them to have the resolve to reach a new destination.

Persistence is an essential part of personal impact. Being focussed and single-minded requires persistence when there is hesitancy or criticism from others. But persistence is not about ignoring the genuine concerns of others. Effective persistence comes from properly addressing the concerns of others and continuing to be clear about what is the right approach.

Persistence involves physical, emotional, intellectual and spiritual stamina. At the heart of persistence there needs to be a resilience to keep going, irregardless of the criticisms and how you are feeling inside.

When there is limited progress we can feel disheartened and our energy can dry up. We sometimes have to put on the "persistence mask". Just as a cyclist going up a steep hill has to keep peddling, regardless of the pain, sometimes in difficult situations we have to keep peddling despite the pain.

It is important that persistence is tempered by reality. There may be a moment to stop and let other events happen before we renew our persistence. There is a time when it is important to acknowledge that we may need to wait for some views to change before our persistence is likely to lead to the right outcome.

Harry was clear that the team needed to plan ahead more effectively and be clearer about the milestones it wanted to reach in six months' time. Harry was not getting much support and thought his persistence was beginning to alienate some of his colleagues. He had put his markers down and felt that he should hold back on expressing his concerns about forward planning.

One or two mishaps occured and the team became less confident about its future direction. Harry reiterated his concern about the need to plan more clearly six months ahead and now received a positive response. Harry was pleased that he had initially been persistent, but had then bided his time and returned to this theme at a judicious moment.

In practice

- Keep observing people who are persistent to see what works and what alienates people.

- Experiment with varying the words you use to see whether packaging your persistence in different ways helps.

- When you believe it is important to be persistent, seek allies who are likely to support your view.

- Recognise when persistence might be alienating others and consciously decide whether to continue or withdraw.

- Keep alert to when changes in other people's expectations mean that the time is right to be persistent again.

DO ASK GOOD QUESTIONS

A GOOD QUESTION that identifies the nub of a problem can be worth 100 times more than a weighty, factual analysis. A thoughtful question can prompt new insights and connections.

The idea

A good question is like a spear that goes straight to the heart. There is no escape from a good question which prompts thought and action. Questions are part of your weapons of influence and impact.

The good questioner does not need to know the answer. But it helps if they are aware of the key considerations and what might be some of the issues. A question about what is possible on what timescale can help elicit key information. A question about doability can bring together the key facts about practicalities. An open-ended question about how someone feels about a particular impending decision can lead to the surfacing of risks and emotions.

Rosanna was new to a big role. She knew very little about the history of the department, its politics or the economic realities they were facing. She asked different people a range of questions and built up a perspective about the successes and vulnerabilities of the organisation's plans. Rosanna was always courteous. She weighed her questions carefully and gave people time to respond, and did not allow them to make half relevant speeches in response to her questions.

Her questions were clear but not relentless. She knew that annoying people by being too forensic with her questions would mean that they would avoid her. Her questions had to help crystallise next steps. Rosanna's aim was to get her colleagues to want her to ask pertinent questions so that it would help crystallise their thinking.

In practice

- Be conscious of the difference between closed questions (which are very explicit) and open questions (which provide starters for discussion).

- Prepare your questions carefully and think about what types of answers would be helpful.

- Do not rush your questions. Give time for your audience to listen to the question and absorb it.

- Recognise that the initial answer to a question may not be the ultimate response.

- Assume that people will often take time to process their response to good questions.

- Ask questions with an openness of heart and a twinkle in your eye – this is much more likely to lead to an open and creative response.

- Do not become too predictable in your use of questions or your effectiveness will diminish.

- Keep a log of the type of questions that work best for you and do not be too modest about using them.

- Do not pad your questions with extraneous information, let the question speak for itself.

- Demonstrate that you have listened to the answers even if you might not agree with them.

27 DO SUMMARISE

IF YOU CAN summarise well you hold the key to unlocking the next steps and ensuring that progress is made. A good summary provides the foundation for the next step.

The idea

The individual who can summarise the key points of a discussion can help bring clarity about a way forward and can be hugely influential.

We may be hesitant to intervene in a complicated or difficult conversation because we do not know the answer that will win everyone's support. What is needed is someone who can summarise the key arguments and crystallise the issues where further consideration is needed.

The summariser has to be careful to sum up the conversation accurately. If your summary appears biased, your credibility will diminish. But as you summarise you can ensure that key points which are particularly important to you are mentioned, provided they are part of an accurate, overall summary.

Olivia had developed a reputation as a good summariser. She was often asked to chair team meetings because she was able to pull together key themes at the end of each meeting. The respect for Olivia's ability to summarise gave her an important influential role within the team. When she was a participant and not the chair, her colleagues would often look to her and invite her to summarise the conversation so far. Olivia recognised that this gave her a significant role which she had to treat with care. She was always respectful of the different type of contributions that colleagues made.

In practice

- As a discussion progresses, note down the two or three key points of agreement and a couple of points where further consideration is needed.

- Be ready to share your summary at an appropriate moment.

- Resist the notion that if you do not have the solution you cannot contribute.

- Draw on the experience of others who summarise well and adopt some of their approaches.

- Do not feel that a summary has to cover every point: a good summary is about catching the essence of the main points.

- Do not feel hurt if your summary is ignored: it will often have fed into people's thinking without their explicitly acknowledging its significance.

DO TRUST YOUR INTUITION

IT IS WELL worth trusting your intuition. It may well be telling you something important when you feel uneasy about a course of action or a decision. It is rarely just irrational.

The idea

We rely on facts and information, but we also rely on our intuition. We sometimes feel fear or unease before we know there is an issue. Similarly, we may sense an opportunity before we have logically considered all the facts.

Our intuition draws on our cultural background, our life experience, our values, our emotions and our experiences. The unconscious part of our brain processes a lot of information and ideas beyond what we are consciously thinking about and can give us valuable insight.

If you are feeling an intuitive sense that now is the time to talk to a particular individual, write a paper or contribute in a particular way, then it is likely that your brain is telling you something. Not all intuitions are accurate; they need to be tested. But our intuition provides us with valuable data that is folly to ignore.

James felt uncomfortable that a particular group of clients were being ignored as the company did its forward planning. He could not put specific reasons to his unease as this client group had become less important over recent years. But he had a strong sense that the views of this particular client group should be taken into account and that they could be more influential in the future than had previously been assumed. His colleagues were disparaging at first, but because they trusted James they took his advice in consulting this client group, whose views were more valuable than they had originally anticipated.

In practice

- Remember when your intuitive sense has given you valuable data in the past.

- Be willing to discuss your intuitions with people you trust to test their validity.

- Treat your intuiton as a valuable source of insight.

- Reflect on what your intuition is telling you – explore it and do not dismiss it.

- Recognise the patterns about when is the best time for you to draw insights from your wider subconscious experience.

29 DO MAKE DECISIONS

WE SHOULD BE making decisions all the time. If we put something off we are making a decision not to decide. We will not get every decision right, but we have to live by our decisions. That is life.

The idea

We make decisions about our approach, our attitude and how we spend our time every day. We may feel that we are swept along by forces outside our control. But even then we can choose how we respond, our attitude of mind and our demeanour.

In order to have any personal impact we need to make decisions. These include how we spend our time and energy, what our priority tasks are, who we build key relationships with, what is the balance between thinking and acting, and how we inter-relate the short-term and the long-term.

Some decisions will be a long time in contemplation. Others will have to be made quickly with limited information. Our personal impact does not come from getting 100% of the decisions right, but getting to a point where most of our decisions prove to be correct. If 80% of the decisions are right, in most spheres of life, we are probably doing fine.

The difficult decisions are often ones where we do not know whether the answer is right quickly. Decisions about long-term investment or employing people or shaping priorities may not be evidently successful for a year or so.

We have to live with our decisions whether they prove to be right or wrong. Accepting that our decisions are sometimes wrong is a part of life. Living with the consequences of bad decisions may not be straightforward, but is never a reason to avoid making decisions.

Chloe was conscious that her team needed to be reduced in size. She needed to let two of her staff go. She thought long and hard about what was the right decision and looked at various criteria that she could apply. The decision in relation to one person was easy as her performance had been indifferent. But there was not much to choose between the rest of her team in terms of performance, although their levels of positive attitude varied. Eventually, Chloe decided who she wanted to let go and had the difficult conversation with both parties. Chloe recognised that her job required her to make such decisions, and that this was a task that had to be done, which she did with thoughtfulness and courtesy.

In practice

- Recognise that you are making decisions every day about your approach, your attitude and your demeanour.

- When you get a decision right acknowledge that you have made a good decision.

- Set aside time during the week to make decisions if this is an approach that helps you.

- Imagine that you have made a particular decision. Put it aside for the moment and see what your reaction is to having made that decision a day later.

- Accept that you will not get every decision right and that the consequences of some decisions will be painful.

- Accept that making decisions is part of your role and something you cannot ignore.

- Give thanks for the privilege and responsibility of being able to make decisions.

30 DO ACKNOWLEDGE SUCCESS

WHEN SOMEONE HAS been successful always acknowledge it – be it a key success for the organisation, or a small personal success for the individual. Acknowledging success helps establish a bond with the individual to whom you have shown appreciation.

The idea

With our busy schedules it is very common for us to move quickly from one activity to another. We solve one problem and move immediately onto the next. We often assume that others also work at a similar pace.

We recognise how much we appreciate positive comments from others when they acknowledge our progress, good contributions or effective outcomes. If someone praises us by identifying what we have done well we are encouraged and that pattern of behaviour is reinforced. The more specific the commendation is, the more likely we are to believe it.

Acknowledging success is one of the simplest ways of enabling others to grow in confidence and effectiveness. Although we may have given words of praise before, it is the repetition that reinforces positive response and behaviour.

Sophie worked hard as a senior nurse and expected everyone else to work as hard as her. She received feedback that she was not acknowledging other people's contributions enough. She recognised the point and began to be much more overt in thanking and praising the nurses who worked for her. Initially she wondered if it was worthwhile, but she enjoyed giving positive comments and noticed that the attitude within her team was becoming more positive. People were more willing to do difficult tasks because they recognised that they would be thanked for their extra contributions.

In practice

- Be willing to give thanks and praise for both small and large tasks.

- Take note of who particularly needs and benefits from thanks and praise.

- Use different ways of recognising success through words, notes and small gifts.

- Ensure that success is recognised across your organisation and not just of those in the most high profile positions.

- Ensure that you obtain feedback from members of your team or organisation to see if they feel that their successes are being appropriately acknowledged.

- When someone acknowledges your success allow yourself to enjoy their appreciation.

- Find reasons to celebrate the success of the team and work out jointly how you can build on that success.

DON'T

31 DON'T GRUMP

As soon as you grump and complain the attitude of those around you changes. They are likely to become more wary of you and less willing to share their reservations or concerns with you.

The idea

When things are not going well it is a natural reaction for us to walk around with a gloomy face. If a number of things have gone wrong the gloomy face might turn into a grump where you begin to complain and look crotchety.

We are all allowed a grump from time to time, but if it becomes a regular pattern those around us will begin to distance themselves from us. If you feel in need of a grump the right thing to do may be to move away from other people and have a private grump. A walk in the fresh air can help us let the grump out and get over it as quickly as possible.

Our grumps tend to have a particular pattern. We are likely to sense when they are about to appear and can develop a mechanism for handling grumps. The grumps tend to disappear after a fairly predictable length of time. When a grump begins to happen, knowing how to handle it can help it disappear quickly.

Most grumps happen because our plans have been thwarted, our predictions misplaced or our efforts have not been appreciated. The more dependent we are on the approval of others the more likely we are to get ourselves into a grumpy situation. If we can assess the value of our contribution, and are less dependent on the approval of others, we are more likely to keep our equilibrium.

There are occasions when a grump is a perfectly reasonable response and can give a powerful signal. If a group of people have not pulled their weight as much as they should and encouragement has not worked, then a premeditated grump might be what is needed to stimulate a team to a higher level of performance.

Joshua knew he had become overly tired and was likely to go into grump mode. He slowed his pace as he came into the office and recognised that he needed to take his work one step at a time. He could sense his irritation rise when two people did not deliver their projects on time. When frustration was about to get the better of him, he went outside for some fresh air. He only allowed his grumpiness to show in the forthcoming week when it was a deliberate response to his team's limited effort in completing a task.

In practice

- Watch your equilibrium to see when you are likely to grump.

- Recognise the pattern of when frustration levels rise and a grump might be about to occur.

- Be willing to move into different environments to counteract a rising grump.

- Recognise the likely life cycle of a grump and plan your day to take account of that.

- Smile at yourself as the grump begins to pass.

- Only allow yourself to show a grump when you are clear there is good reason to do so and it is likely to have a beneficial effect.

32 DON'T BE A VICTIM

When you allow yourself to be a victim you begin to think you are to blame and have been forced into a situation for which you are not accountable. Remember that you always have choices.

The idea

We can all feel like a victim of circumstances. We may feel that we are losing out for a wide range of possible reasons, such as: my boss does not like me, I am under appreciated, my experience is not valued, a misjudgement of a few years ago has never been forgotten, I went to the wrong school, I was brought up in the wrong country or I did not have the right type of education or training.

We can sometimes enjoy being a victim and blaming other people for our woes. It may be true that judgements have gone against us or that the attitude of others towards us is unfair, but we are not helping ourselves if we regard ourselves as a victim. We can easily lose heart and feel powerless, and indulge in blaming everybody else for our woes.

Beginning to feel like a victim is akin to the first sign of an infectious disease that needs to be tackled quickly so it does not spread. We need to turn it round before it takes hold of us. We can take control of a situation by remembering the choices we have and by reminding ourselves of our strengths and advantages so we are not deterred by feelings of adversity. When I had a detached retina there was a risk that I would feel sorry for myself and feel like a victim as I had to cancel a walking holiday. My response was to tell myself that I now had some precious days when I had to sit still: I now had the time and energy to dictate this book. This book would never have happened if I had allowed myself to feel like a victim because of a detached retina.

In the face of adversity, instead of feeling like a victim, ask yourself what type of opportunity it provides to either learn new things, build new relationships or to do things differently.

Amelia felt hard done by because she had not been promoted. She began to feel victimised because of her size, tone of voice, experience, limited education and facial expressions. It was her partner who told her to stop feeling like a victim and get on with life. After feedback from the promotion interview she recognised what she needed to do to improve her experience and performance. She felt less like a victim and began to work constructively to prepare for the next promotion board. Amelia was grateful to her partner who had prised her out of her victim mode.

In practice

- Recognise when you might feel like a victim.

- Laugh at yourself when the victim mode grips you.

- Ask friends to tell you when you get into victim mode and know who can help lift yourself out of that state of mind.

- Be alert to other people going into victim mode – as you help them move out of that mode you are giving yourself the same practical lessons.

33 DON'T BANG ON

KNOWING WHEN TO speak and when to stop is an important skill. Banging on about a particular subject can be counter-productive without us realising that our unrelenting focus is causing us to lose support.

The idea

When we feel strongly about something we want to be persistent and ensure we get our point across. Persistence can be a great strength, but also a liability. What matters is the persistence of intent rather than persistence of action. Sometimes a tactical withdrawal is the best response.

Repetition is sometimes needed as many of us only take in a certain proportion of what is said and we need to hear a message a number of times to get its full impact. But the person who is unrelenting and always using the same phrases can become a turn off.

When we are tempted to keep banging on about a particular point it may be time to change our approach. Perhaps we need to talk individually with colleagues rather than continually highlighting a point in meetings. Or perhaps we need to collect more evidence to prove a point, or ask questions that enable others to reach similar conclusions.

If we feel strongly about a subject there is a risk that we might speak in the same tone of voice. A repetitive tone can become harsh after a while. If we vary the tone, pace and timbre in which the message is said then we will come across as more melodic and people may be more willing to listen to us. A melodic voice is easier to listen to and can produce a more sympathetic reaction in the listener.

Thomas was felt passionately that the college needed to introduce a course in a particular area. He used every opportunity to press the case relentlessly for this course. He thought that using the same arguments and the same examples would enable him to build a credible case. After a while Thomas realised that he needed to vary his approach and pitch. He talked to a range of different staff to get them on his side and he sought the support of students and companies who used the services of the college. He used a repertoire of approaches and eventually the key committee decided to introduce this course. Thomas' case was helped by the fact he had stopped banging on about the matter and was now relying much more on influencing individuals about the wider benefits of this programme.

In practice

- Beware if you are always speaking at the same volume and in the same tone.

- Be deliberate about when you are repetitive and observe what effect it is has.

- When you want to be persistent, use a range of different approaches so your persistence is not regarded as blinkered.

- When you feel strongly about something and want to make a strongly-worded speech, choose your words deliberately and be mindful about what is happening to your emotions.

- Be ready to pause and wait for an opportune moment to come back into the fray.

34 | DON'T SHOUT

THE INDIVIDUAL WHO shouts and bawls and shows uncontrolled anger will lose credibility instantly and look out of control. Always keep calm and, if you raise your voice, do it consciously and deliberately.

The idea

If you are about to lose your cool and shout, don't. When the frustration level reaches that intensity, stop and take a time-out. This gives you time to regroup and recognise where your emotions are taking you.

In some situations you may want to express strong and clear views. You may deliberately be raising your voice to a slightly higher pitch. But if you shout others are likely to either shout back, or declare your behaviour to be out of bounds, or sit there seething or quietly withdraw. The understanding colleague or member of staff will withdraw and let you cool down. But others might see this as an opportunity take advantage of your anger, so beware that when you shout you might be at your most vulnerable.

When we want to shout out loud, it is because there is something that we are cross or outraged about. Harnessing anger and frustration and turning it to positive effect can produce enormous energy to change the course of events and correct unfairness. Anger that is unharnessed can be destructive to you and those around you and undermines the impact you might otherwise have.

When you shout you create enemies who would happily see you fail. If you demean people by raising your voice at them, or by declaring a piece of work to be of no value, you risk of killing off their motivation and any sense of loyalty.

Jessica was known for her fiery temper. Her father had been in the Forces and used colourful language on a regular basis. Jessica had grown up with this pattern of behaviour and would raise her voice if she did not get what she wanted. As the manager in a departmental store, she achieved some success by ordering her staff around. But they were fearful of being shouted at and did not want to stay working in her department for long. Jessica knew that if she wanted to keep her staff she needed to change the way she reacted to them. She learnt that when she wanted to shout at them, she should move into a different space and calm down. Gradually she saw the benefits of a more calm approach but knew she would have to control her fiery temperament.

In practice

- Be aware of the pitch of your voice.

- If you want to shout at someone, take a time-out first and decide whether that is really the right solution and what you want to do.

- Understand the pattern of when you might feel angry and want to shout, and know how you best handle those feelings.

- Use raising your voice as a deliberate technique when you want to show the strength of your concerns.

- Have one or two trusted others in the workplace who you can talk to when you want to shout.

DON'T LET YOUR EMOTIONS GET THE BETTER OF YOU

WE CAN USE our emotions to influence others but if we are not in control of our emotions we can overwhelm others and undermine the support we have built up.

The idea

Our emotions give us valuable data about what is happening above and below the surface. They can tell us whether an organisation is happy or stressed, purposeful or lost. When we walk into a room our emotions tell us about the energy level and whether the tenor of the people is more negative or positive. For engagement to be successful we need to respond to those emotions we are experiencing. Where there is lightness we can respond to the humour, where there is serious intent we can allow our intellectual curiosity to follow and contribute to the debate.

Emotions can be the best of friends but they can be double-edged. Our emotional reactions can mean we are more critical of someone than we should be because of their voice or looks or sense of superiority. Our emotions can lead us to dismiss someone for extraneous reasons unrelated to the quality of their contribution. Resentment, anger or disdain can often well up within us and hijack our emotions so that rational thought goes out the window.

Bob did not agree with a particular course of action and began to speak quickly and vehemently as he criticised it. His emotive arguments were initially attractive but were soon seen as resentment because his preferred approach was not winning people over. Eventually he backed down from the argument, having lost all his allies.

In practice

- Observe your emotions in any situation. Recognise the patterns and use them as valuable information when tackling subsequent situations.

- Recognise the emotions in any situation and judge how far you want to go along with those emotional reactions or try to change their direction.

- Recognise when there is a strength of emotion in you that is giving you the passion to be influential and make a difference.

- Recognise when your emotional reaction is so strong that it might be blinding you to the reality of the situation and mean you are disregarding good points made by others.

- When you feel that your emotional reactions are likely to be overwhelming, decide how to withdraw judiciously to get a hold of your emotions and how you ought to react.

- Be sensitive to when your emotional reactions are being counter-productive and causing you to lose support.

36 DON'T DISAPPEAR

WHEN THE HEAT is on and your presence is needed, don't just disappear, but at the same time recognise that you will need some private space to consider the next steps to take.

The idea

Most people get used to seeing their leader around. They may not see you often but they will observe a pattern about when you are there and when you are not around. If you disappear for a long period, this will arouse curiosity and interest. The rumour mill will soon be active. Have you disappeared because you have lost interest or have other priorities, or you are indisposed or are about to get the sack? If you about to disappear for a period, it is worth letting people know why so they are not unsettled by your absence. If you are away on a sequence of visits, letting people know why you are away and later sharing what you have learnt from your visits can both satisfy their curiosity and bring new insights into the organisation.

The people who work for you will be watching you all the time. If you work in an open plan office that is both a plus and a minus. They will pick up on your energy and your desire to do the job well. They will also pick up your uncertainty or unease if it shows in your voice and your actions.

Sometimes it is absolutely right to disappear and have time on your own, or with a coach or with other trusted others. Space to reflect privately is precious. It is important to have rules about when and how you can be contacted when you have deliberately disappeared.

For example you may have commited yourself to not read e-mails, but you might say that you will look at urgent text messages.

Daniel was leading a major project for an architect's firm. In the early stages he was very visible as he offered guidance and steered the project. All of a sudden he disappeared and moved onto a different assignment. The architects on the original project were disconcerted that he had disappeared so quickly. Daniel soon realised that he should have explained why he was moving onto a different assignment. He explained the importance of the new assignment to the firm and agreed to be contactable for advice on the original project at key points. Daniel had learnt from this experience to be careful not to appear to disappear too quickly in the future and recognised the need to explain what was happening and why.

In practice

- Be mindful that you are being observed continuously by your staff and colleagues.

- Be conscious when you might inadvertently disappear and your colleagues will be left wondering what you are doing.

- Let people know what you are spending your time away doing, and demonstrate the benefits of that experience.

- Create time to disappear and use that time purposefully.

- Be mindful of what your emotions are saying when you feel the need to disappear.

37   DON'T PANIC

PANIC SPREADS LIKE wildfire. Part of personal impact is the ability to keep calm and not panic or appear over-anxous.

The idea

In a crisis the most influential people are those who keep calm and are clear-minded. We may feel anxious and uptight inside, but if we display anxiety we create unease and inhibit the ability to reach a measured and clear outcome.

If we appear to be panicking those around us may rapidly move into panic mode. If we look calm and collected, there is a reasonable prospect that those around us will become calmer and more collected. When we panic we make rash, instant decisions. If we look calm but are still weighing the considerations in a seemingly clear way, then we can be very influential. In a crisis situation when somebody can say from previous experience that the right next steps to take are 'X' and 'Y', they are likely to be taken seriously. Their advice is likely to be followed in the absence of other clear views about the possible next steps to take.

If you build up a reputation for keeping calm and not panicking, this becomes a part of how you will be viewed within the organisation. An individual who has a reputation for both calmness and being in control of themselves in stressful situations is welcome in any team.

Ella's team always seemed to be panicking prior to deadlines. Tempers got frayed and irrational behaviours came to the fore. Ella was determined not to be part of this panicking. She deliberately kept calm and stayed clear of some of the panic-ridden conversations. She was always clear about how she was going to contribute and always delivered her goals. Her calmness and measuredness made her ever more influential. The team leader sought her advice about how the team might plan more effectively and keep calm more readily. Her quiet words of advice were gradually embedded into the way the team approached situations, and the sense of panic gradually diminished.

In practice

- Observe what are the flash points that create panic.

- Observe how others handle a crisis situation in either a good or bad way.

- Remember how damaging it is to your personal reputation and impact to panic.

- Recognise the different techniques that work for you to keep calm and measured in panic situations.

- When you are in danger of becoming over anxious, try to step back from the situation and reflect on what keeps you calm and maintains your equilibrium.

38 DON'T GOSSIP

Don't gossip because it always come back to bite you. Gossip is insidious and undermines trust.

The idea

Most of us are intrigued to hear gossip about other people, but find it distasteful and hateful if we are gossiped about. If we gossip about people to others it will legitimise other people gossiping about us.

When an individual has made a valuable contribution you might say to a number of people how much you appreciate their contribution. This a positive form of passing messages around an organisation. Even then, people may draw a distinction between who you are being positive about and who you are silent about. So even words of praise have to be expressed with care, so they are related specifically to a distinctive contribution.

If you gossip about the bosses it is quite likely to get back to them that you have been expressing views about them. In one sense that is fair game, but as soon as you are critical about a boss that perspective can be magnified as it is passed on. You might have suggested that a speech given by the boss was not their best. By the time your comments reach the boss your initial comment might have become magnified to the boss never being any good at public speaking. The best way of avoiding a damaging rumour is to not say anything that is potentially critical in the first place.

The most dangerous form of gossip is about someone's personal life. It is best to stay well away from anything to do with such. What matters is the nature of their contribution in the work environment and their integrity in that setting. If you participate in gossip about what they do outside work it undermines your integrity.

Someone's personal impact is strongly enhanced if they have a reputation for keeping confidences and not gossiping. If people know they can trust you to keep confidential issues they talk through with you, then you are likely to become a trusted and respected mentor.

Lucy enjoyed talking with her friends at work about a range of different things. When they went for a drink after work the conversation about their fellow colleagues could become quite blunt. Lucy was wary about loose talk. She always took the view that she would never say anything about somebody that she would not say to their face. This proved to be a very good guideline which stopped her from becoming part of a gossiping network.

In practice

- Choose your words carefully when you talk about people.

- Always assume that anything you say about an individual will get back to them.

- See speaking positively about people as a potentially constructive means of disseminating good messages, but be mindful that people will distinguish between who you talk positively about and who you do not comment upon.

- Be aware of getting into situations where you feel under pressure to join in the gossip.

- Be willing to sit above gossip and not join in and do not believe most of the gossip you hear.

39 DON'T DELAY UNNECCESSARILY

WHEN YOU ARE clear what is the right thing to do or say, after taking a short while to double-check your perspective, don't delay your action unnecessarily.

The idea

The search for perfection can be a major inhibitor. We are constantly searching for the best answer, but sometimes the solution just needs to be good enough – it does not have to be perfect.

There is sometimes an opportune moment when people are more open to persuasion about a particular course of action, or when you are more likely to get a positive response about a new initiative. When the time is right we need to act and not delay. This is not about rushing into action without first considering the options. It is about thinking clearly about what is the right thing to do, taking stock of the situation, and then taking action. Personal impact is always enhanced if you build a reputation for bringing clarity about the next steps to take, demonstrate the ability to review the situation quickly and carefully, and then take decisive action.

Sometimes we feel that there will always be a better answer. We want more evidence and analysis and to consider the views of a wider range of people. All of these aspirations are worthy and desirable, but not if we lose momentum to the point where the final decision becomes irrelevant. We may ponder long and hard about whether to apply for a particular job but if we delay beyond the closing date, our decision is irrelevant. If we procrastinate about a particular business opportunity it is quite likely that someone else will enter the market and take the opportunity from us.

Charlotte wanted to become a Deputy Head of a school. She knew that she had to widen her knowledge and experience if she was going to become a serious candidate when the Deputy Head position at her school became available, but she decided that it could wait and focussed on her day job instead. When the Deputy Head job became available she applied for the position but her application seemed thin because of her narrow focus. Charlotte had unnecessarily delayed her wider preparation, which meant that she was not a serious candidate when the opportunity arose. Charlotte recognised that she would have to prepare more thoroughly if she was going to become a candidate for a future Deputy Head post.

In practice

- Carefully consider the action you want to take and its timing and the inter-relation between the two.

- Remember that to delay is to make a decision.

- Think as objectively as you can about the right action and the right timing for it.

- When you are inclined to delay an action think carefully about your options before you conclude that it is the right thing to do.

- Accept that delaying a decision is sometimes right as problems can solve themselves if they are left alone for a while.

40 DON'T GIVE UP

THERE ARE TIMES when we want to throw our hands in the air and give up. It may be right to channel our energy in new directions, but giving up and losing heart can be self-destructive.

The idea

Our personal impact is enhanced by our determination and persistence. Sometimes we get stuck and it can feel as if there is nowhere to go. There is a danger that we may lose heart, our confidence saps and the energy that we possess dissipates.

When we encounter an obstacle we may decide to go around it, over it or under it, but if we give up the obstacle is still there. When there is a barrier that seems insurmountable there may be different ways of tackling it. Perhaps we need to seek different sources of advice, or join forces with other people and tackle a barrier with the combined effort.

If we look as if we have given up we may not be given similar projects or tasks again. But if we show that we can adapt to a situation, we then become known for our responsiveness and adaptability. Giving up implies defeat and dejection, while changing direction, learning from experience and refocusing energy builds and maintains our confidence and credibility and does not undermine it.

Some projects do need to be aborted, but not because people have given up. When projects are aborted it carries much more credibility if the change is based on the consideration of new evidence and the best use of resources. Those leading the project can then move on with their reputation enhanced rather than diminished.

George was mortified that all the work he had put into an engineering design looked as if it would be wasted. The purchaser was beginning to lose interest. The easiest thing for George to do was to give up on the whole project. But he knew that this reaction would be bad for his reputation and his well-being. He talked to the client and reached an agreement that the project could potentially be saved if the approach was radically changed. George was not going to give up on this project easily and agreed to a reshaping to meet the client's wishes.

In practice

- Be mindful when your energy begins to wane and you feel like giving up.

- Recognise what effect the desire to give up has on your energy and commitment levels.

- Look at ways in which the desire to give up can be converted into a resolve to get around obstacles.

- See barriers as opportunities to do things differently rather than to give up.

- Remember to reframe giving up as a strategic withdrawal in the light of new evidence.

DEMONSTRATE

41 DEMONSTRATE LOYALTY

LOYALTY IS ABOUT demonstrating your continued willingness to support wholeheartedly those who are leading you and the cause for which you both stand.

The idea

Soldiers pride themselves on loyalty to their regiment. This sense of loyalty reinforces their resolve to keep going, however difficult the battle and however arduous the marching. Loyalty to a cause is a powerful motivator which generates resolve, energy and resilience. Individuals may feel a strong sense of loyalty to their employer, their boss, the cause which they are associated with and the people they are trying to help.

A boss should always be keeping an eye on who is loyal to them and who might be turning their attentions elsewhere. If you want to influence your boss, being explicit about your loyalty reassures your boss, who is then likely to listen to you more carefully.

Loyalty is a trait many bosses treasure in their staff. But they may become a little concerned if what they sense is blind loyalty. An attitude of loyalty that always sees the boss as being perfect can lead to poor decisions. If someone is surrounded by those who are blindly loyal and think their boss can do no wrong, this can lead to delusions of grandeur and a blindness to impending disasters.

Loyalty is important up to a point but blind loyalty can be myopic and destructive. Personal impact with some people depends on your being able to demonstrate your loyalty to them, but the best type of loyalty tells "truth to power" as well as brings a high level of practical support. Loyalty to a particular cause is fine, provided the cause has not become outdated or irrelevant.

William felt a strong sense of loyalty to his boss who had appointed him to his current role, but there were moments when he felt his boss was misguided. Did he express complete support for him on those occasions or did William tell his boss that he had concerns? William decided that in public he would be completely loyal to his boss. In private William began to share his reservations with his boss about some of the decisions he had taken. The fact that William was loyal in public but willing to be open and critical in private meant that his boss took William's views seriously and began to adjust some of his approaches.

In practice

- Who are you particularly loyal to, and what are the reasons for that loyalty?

- Is that loyalty always expressed in the most constructive of ways, or should you be more willing to express reservations?

- How do you balance being loyal publicly and speaking "truth to power" in private?

- Does loyalty sometimes get in the way of reaching good decisions?

42 DEMONSTRATE RESPECT

DEMONSTRATING RESPECT IS about acknowledging and seeking to understand the different cultural perspectives that people bring and not demeaning them.

The idea

Our personal impact is enhanced when we show a clear respect for different interests and perspectives. Showing respect is about taking the trouble to find out about people's values and qualities. It is acknowledging cultural differences and respecting why people from various cultures view and handle issues differently.

Showing respect includes recognising the importance of religious beliefs in a person's perspective, and acknowledging religious practices that individuals and communities see as important and not dismissing or undermining them. It is about talking with others about their religious background and perspective with genuine interest and respect.

Showing respect is often about acknowledging international differences. It is recognising that different nations and cultures have different expectations and ways of making decisions. Respect for the heritage of a nation is paramount if you are going to influence and be respected by people from that nation. Respect is a two-way process. The more you respect other people's backgrounds and traditions, the more likely they are to respect yours. Being willing to share something of your own cultural, social and religious background helps build mutual respect that can provide a sound basis if you then need to move into negotiation.

Phoebe had bracketed everyone from India as owners of restaurants. When Phoebe began to work with a couple of IT specialists from India she was astounded by their confidence and their ability to translate ideas into action. Her respect for them and the Indian culture grew quickly and she was now clearer that her personal impact depended on respecting people irrespective of their cultural background.

In practice

- Are there groups you respect more than others? Is that justified?

- How might you build an even stronger sense of respect for some people you have tended to dismiss?

- How might strengthening your understanding and respect of particular people enable you to influence them more effectively?

- Can you build a stronger sense of mutual respect in order to reinforce a sense of mutual influence which is constructive and two-way?

43 DEMONSTRATE YOU UNDERSTAND

IF WE DEMONSTRATE that we understand the people we are dealing with, they are more likely to talk freely and be open to be influenced. If we do not show we understand, we may be regarded as irrelevant.

The idea

When I work as a coach with someone in a new business area I need to demonstrate that I understand the issues faced in that industry. I need to have enough understanding to ask the right questions and be clear about the priorities and key concerns. For example, anyone bringing marketing advice to an organisation has to understand enough about both the market, the company and its people before they can offer constructive advice that is influential.

Unless you are seen to understand the nuances of the world you want to enter, you are unlikely to be invited in with open arms. Building up understanding of an organisation is invariably at a number of different levels. The initial basis is a clear grounding in factual knowledge and an awareness of trends, followed by knowledge about an organisation's history, its successes, failures and aspirations. The next level is about understanding the emotions behind why people are part of the organisation, what drives them and what they are trying to achieve. A good understanding starts with facts, then trends, then aspirations and then hopes and fears.

You can show your understanding in fairly simple ways. Asking pertinent questions always helps, followed by showing you understand some of the history and know about the organisation's past successes. Those skilled in international diplomacy have developed well-honed techniques in acknowledging their understanding of national and organisational history and culture. Embodying the diplomat skills of demonstrating that you understand is part of reinforcing your personal impact.

Samuel was frustrated by the rigid rules of the government department he was working with. He decided he needed to understand where these rules came from and how they applied. His counterpart in the government department talked him through the reasons for the procurement and audit rules. Samuel was not convinced about the merits of these arrangements, but because he now understood why they were there he was less frustrated by them. He was now able to stop his personal frustration from getting in the way of his working relationship with his colleagues.

In practice

- Take time to understand the facts, history and aspirations of organisations you are working with.

- Be willing to find out more about the organisation by asking thoughtful questions.

- Be willing to demonstrate your understanding by contributing in discussions.

- Remember that giving evidence that you understand aspirations and hopes means that others will be more open to your influence.

DEMONSTRATE DEFERENCE BUT NOT TOO MUCH

SHOWING DEFERENCE IS proper recognition of someone's status. But too much deference can mean you become ineffectual and lose the personal impact that you might otherwise have had.

The idea

Someone who has worked hard to reach a particular level deserves deference as an acknowledgement of their hard work and status. Deference to a leader is needed to ensure that there is order and that decisions can be made. Not showing deference can lead to aggravation and discord, and sometimes even anarchy.

Sometimes deference is to the position someone holds rather than necessarily to the person in that position. The judge in a court room demands deference by virtue of their role so that order and discipline prevail in court proceedings. We need to work within the systems that any organisation runs itself by and show deference to those in positions of responsibility in order to build our credibility and a role for ourselves.

But demonstrating too much deference can be ineffectual. Once we have shown a reasonable degree of deference to our seniors and built up a relationship of respect, we may well have the freedom to say where we think their approach could benefit from being changed.

The most constructive working relationships are those with a mutual exchange of views and perspectives in a thoughtful and purposeful way regardless of position or rank.

Alice was conscious that she owed a lot to her boss, Fred. She respected Fred's knowledge and ability and was deferential towards him, but was concerned that her deference was getting in the way of frank conversation. After discussing this issue openly with Fred, Alice was relieved at his encouragement and invitation for her to be more challenging and open in their conversations.

In practice

- Reflect on the reasons for the deference you show to some individuals: is it stuck in a time warp?

- Consider whether your deference gets in the way of your being able to say what you think.

- How might you turn a relationship that is too deferential into one that is more constructive and purposeful?

- What are the changes you need to make to ensure your deference is not undermining your personal impact?

- Who might you decide to be deliberately less deferential towards?

45 DEMONSTRATE YOU REMEMBER

DEMONSTRATING THAT YOU remember details builds credibility with the people you are seeking to influence and have an impact upon. The fact that you remember shows your serious interest and the impact someone has had on you.

The idea

Our minds are full of clutter – sometimes we remember names and places, and on other occasions we forget them or leave them behind.

But remembering past events or recalling the occasion when you met can provide a valuable bridge between the past and present and help create a sense of being on the same page or wanting to work together in a constructive way.

As an executive coach I normally send my coachees a note after a meeting that provides a prompt for the action they have said they are going to take. It is also how I go into the next meeting remembering what our previous discussion had covered, which then helps to frame my coaching questions. Part of my job as an executive coach is to be on the same page as my coachee. Therefore, I need to remember their context and perspectives from our last exchange.

Demonstrating you remember is not about memorising every detail, but about keeping in mind key facts or incidents and bringing them into future discussion. It is worth spending a few moments recalling those memories before meeting somebody whom you have not seen or spoken to for a while.

Sometimes your credibility depends on demonstrating that you remember lessons learnt from the past. Demonstrating results after careful reflection of past experience builds credibility about your knowledge and depth of experience.

Alexander thought he recognised the name of the local official he was due to meet to discuss a possible planning application from the charity that he worked for. He wondered whether they had played in the same football team ten years ago. When Alexander shook hands with the official he recognised the centre forward who now had grey hair. There was a smile on both of their faces and they talked about football matches they remembered. Alexander acknowledged the official's footballing skills and recalled two or three of his goals.

When they started their discussion about the planning application, no further reference was made to football. The meeting was business-like but because Alexander had demonstrated that he had remembered their previous meetings, he probably received a fuller explanation of the background and a greater openness to consider a range of different alternatives before a final decision was made.

In practice

- See your memories as valuable stories rather than unnecessary clutter.

- Draw on your memories of what has gone well or less well to provide lessons you can use in influencing others.

- When you do remember someone do not be too shy in recalling those memories with them, but always do it in a positive and warm way.

- Never try to use past, shared experiences in a manipulative way – just allow it to influence the openness and warmth of an exchange.

46 DEMONSTRATE YOU ARE LISTENING

DEMONSTRATING THAT WE are listening shows that we are fully engaged with the people around us and able to contribute in a way that will command respect.

The idea

Good listeners always show that they are listening. They indicate acknowledgement through facial expressions that convey warmth and empathy as well as a shared sense of journeying together.

Good listeners occasionally summarise what they have heard, ask questions that indicate that they recognise the issues and identify ways forward.

The person who can crystallise the range of views they have listened to can provide quality input towards a conversation or strategy. The more you can show that you are listening to a wide range of voices, the more you will garner about people's perceptions. This will strengthen your personal impact because you are acting as a valuable and accurate filter.

Lola was concerned that she was sometimes ignored by the senior people in the department and felt that they considered her to be lightweight and irrelevant. She decided to make her mark by being an active listener. She listened to what the bosses wanted to achieve. Lola listened attentively to clients, to other people in the organisation and to what external consultants were saying about their department. She began to vocalise boldly what she had heard in these conversations. Her bosses began to listen to her now because she had listened to a wide range of people and was able to summarise views with clarity. She became far more influential than she had ever anticipated.

In practice

- Keep demonstrating that you are a good listener through your eyes and facial expressions.

- Keep listening to a wide range of different people and calibrate their perceptions.

- Be willing to crystallise what you have heard and do not hesitate if people appear not to be listening.

- Recognise that if you listen well most people will mirror your facial expressions and respond 'like with like'.

DEMONSTRATE COURTESY

PRACTICING SIMPLE COURTESIES creates a sense of order and respect and gives a powerful, positive first impression. When common courtesies disappear behaviours can rapidly degenerate.

The idea

When I had the operation recently for a detached retina I was under a local anaesthetic and my good eye was covered. I could see none of the action but could hear everything. The surgeon was a model of courtesy and was polite and calm throughout. He was polite whenever he asked for an instrument and said thank you each time he was given anything. The conversation was entirely focussed on the operation and it was purposeful, calm and courteous throughout. What struck me from this example was how important courtesy is in setting the tone for any engagement. The staff and I were relaxed because of the consultant's behaviour.

Common courtesies such as saying please and thank you set a tone for any meeting or exchange. When someone enters a building and observes common courtesies shown between all staff, irrespective of grade or seniority, they are likely to feel positively towards the place and that it is somewhere where they can feel at home.

Politeness does not cost us anything and at the same time builds up our credibility and therefore our opportunity for personal impact and influence within an organisation. In one particular organisation, feedback is always requested from the receptionist who meets interviewees at the front door to see how the potential candidates have treated the people they met.

Max felt a bit aggrieved. He was upset that his bid to do a major piece of work for an international contractor had been turned down. He wanted to be abrupt and rude to others, but something reminded him that this would be a cheap way of showing his disappointment. He decided to be even more courteous to the junior staff and to visitors in order to correct the fact that he was feeling hard done by.

In practice

- Reflect on how people who are always courteous influence you.

- Consider your usual level of courtesy and politeness and what happens when you are in a stressful situation.

- Decide what form of courtesy you want to reinforce in yourself and how to ensure you stick to those expectations.

- Know how you will forewarn yourself when your courtesy standards slip.

48 DEMONSTRATE YOU CARE ABOUT YOUR PEOPLE

DEMONSTRATING THAT YOU genuinely care about your people can produce a level of personal commitment to you and help build a wider reputation for you as someone who cares about others and is worth listening to.

The idea

You will always show interest in the well-being of family members. If you are part of a church or a community group or a club you will want to show genuine interest in the well-being of group members. In a work context, our expressions of caring may be only skin deep – asking a platitudinous question that is rapidly followed by a request to do a piece of work.

Remembering to ask after an ill member of someone's family can be a genuine expression of caring towards a colleague. Remembering birthdays is part of respecting each other as equals within the same community.

The more we show genuine care for those around us, the more they will feel a commitment to us which increases both our personal impact and the impact of the whole team. But showing you care should never be done because it is in your business interest to do so. If that is your rationale it will not last long. Showing you care is a form of genuine kindness and of being part of the same community.

Your impact and influence in an organisation will depend in part on your reputation in the way you care for your staff. If you are seen as being too tough or too soft, there may be reservations about the way you lead. The best advocates for you are those who have experienced your care and your challenge, and have benefited as a consequence.

Molly was often oblivious to the circumstances of her staff, but when Raisa told her that she had cancer Molly was distraught that she had not recognised some of the signs. Molly was now much more vigilant in taking an interest in Raisa's well-being. She was more observant about the well-being of other members of her staff and more conscious of the constructive impact she could have through taking a personal interest while at the same time being rigorous about the performance standards that needed to be met. Molly now tried to set aside some time to ask questions about the well-being of individual members of staff. As a result her interest in people and how they ticked became stronger. Her staff felt closer to her and trusted her more.

In practice

- How much do you care about your people?

- Do you need to care a bit more or a bit less about their well-being?

- How might you show that your care is genuine and not contrived?

- How best do you balance expressing genuine care for your people and getting the work done in an expeditious way?

- With whom do you want to take practical steps to demonstrate the nature of your care for them?

49 DEMONSTRATE YOU ARE INFLUENTIAL

THE MORE INFLUENTIAL you are, the more influential you become. As you demonstrate that you are influential others will seek you out and want to influence you towards their way of thinking.

The idea

When someone is seen to be influential other people will want to listen to them and in turn seek to influence them because they are influential. How do you become part of this virtuous circle in which the consequence of your becoming influential is that you become more influential still?

When I was Director General for Finance for a UK government department it was part of my job to be influential with the Treasury and a range of government departments. My credibility depended on reaching agreement with key parties which were consistent with the interests of the department I worked for.

Being seen to be influential depended on the quality of the relationships I was able to establish with other key interlocutors. Success was not about winning every battle, but about having a constructive dialogue in which I made good points that were listened to, and about reaching conclusions that took my perspectives into account.

When you are influential you can normally rely on other people to draw attention to what you have been able to deliver. It is sometimes beneficial to summarise the outcomes which you have been able to influence, perhaps as part of a regular stocktake. This does not involve shouting about your successes from the hilltops, but is about ensuring in a quiet and consistent way that people are aware of what you have moved forward and helped to deliver.

When people begin to seek your perspective you know that you have begun to be regarded as influential. When your advice is asked for, try to give of your time so that you can reinforce the type of relationship whereby people want to seek your views.

When another person proposes a way forward which you have helped influence, it does not matter if this proposal is not attributed to you. As long as it becomes known that you are a source of advice for a number of people that itself will build your reputation, although some acknowledgement of your contribution is always going to be appreciated.

Benjamin was happy to act as an adviser. He enjoyed chatting through other people's issues and expressing his perspectives. He sought not to be dogmatic and instead responded to what he heard, enabling others to crystallise their own next steps to take. Benjamin did not realise how influential he had become until a couple of people described him as a 'guru'. He was happy to be teased about his 'guru' qualities as this demonstrated the seriousness with which his contribution was now viewed.

In practice

- Be conscious of the different ways in which you influence people.

- Allow people to draw from your thoughts and ideas, suggesting that they might acknowledge your support in some modest way.

- Periodically, do a stocktake that sets out what you and your team have been able to deliver.

- Accept that the most powerful way in which you can create sustained influence is by enabling others to reach their own conclusions.

50 DEMONSTRATE YOUR COMMITMENT

SHOWING THAT YOU are committed to a particular activity or outcome engenders commitment in others, thereby reinforcing your personal impact. When you are less commited, this will be evident to people who know you well.

The idea

When we are committed to a particular enterprise, our enthusiasm and vigour shines through. This type of commitment is contagious and our followers are more likely to adopt a similar attitude.

We show our commitment through both our actions and our words. Our level of commitment can be perceived through the expressions on our faces. Commitment is not about frenetic activity, but rather a steadfastness of resolve and the ability to work through setbacks and not let them undermine your confidence or convictions.

Commitment is about the quality of your contribution and not necessarily the quantity. Commitment does not require us to work 24 hours a day, 7 days a week. It does require us to be focussed on the task in hand and to draw boundaries between work and other activities in a way that reinforces our commitment to different areas of our life.

If commitment to our work begins to waiver, our confidence might diminish and our ability to make tough decisions will certainly be affected. The drop in commitment will be obvious after a while to those who know us well and can have a negative impact.

When our commitment does wane, as it inevitably will from time to time, it is important to be honest with ourselves and perhaps our trusted members in the team about what is happening. Honest conversations with close colleagues can create a new sense of commitment or a passing of the baton to others more committed to taking the endeavour forward.

Effective commitment is about bringing intellectual and emotional energy, but not at all costs. Those who have the biggest impact are those who are committed to their work but are also able to take a break and enjoy other activities so that they return to work refreshed and rejuvenated.

Katherine was working for an international publishing house. She was committed to commission and produce top quality business books but she was perhaps overly biased to the merits of some North American writers. Katherine began to recognise that she needed to widen the range of authors from Europe and Asia and gradually built up a wider group of outstanding authors. The authors knew that Katherine was committed to their endeavour. Two of the authors had opportunities to write for better known publishers but stayed with this publishing house because of Katherine's commitment to their titles.

In practice

- Be clear what you are committed to and what you are lukewarm about.

- Be willing to share that commitment with others in a way which enthuses them and does not suppress their energy.

- Be mindful when your level of commitment might be diminishing and share your concerns with trusted others.

- Recognise that your commitment will in turn generate commitment in others.

- Ensure that the reasons for your commitment are well founded.

51 SHARE YOUR HOPES

SHARING YOUR HOPES helps to create a sense of aspiration. As you share your personal hopes and what matters to you, this can create a desire in others to want to encourage and support you.

The idea

Being authentic means sharing your hopes and fears. It involves revealing what you are passionate about and what your aspirations are for yourself and the people you work with. When you share your hopes you are showing a vulnerability because those hopes might not materialise. But those hopes might also inspire others, and as you set off to fulfil them, others may well follow behind you.

Hopes are different from objectives and serve a different purpose. Objectives are about focussed outcomes to which there is a strong commitment to deliver. Hopes are aspirations that colour the direction you travel in but are not as hard and fast as objectives.

As we share our hopes with others we may spark their imagination. Ideas for capital projects often begin from general aspirations that then turn into plans and grow into impressive outcomes.

As you share hopes and aspirations you do not know whether they will materialise. Many will fall by the wayside. Some hopes will take on a life of their own.

Sometimes we can be hesitant to share our hopes with others because we think they are not soundly based and we may not be able to articulate all the evidence in support of them. But being bold enough to share our hopes is part of the way we can contribute.

Gleaning from others what their hopes are can create a collection of ideas that may develop into something beyond individual hopes and become the shared aspirations of a wider group.

Henry hoped that the scout pack might be able to move to a different building. He had reservations about expressing this hope because he thought it would imply he was dissatisfied with the current arrangements and not loyal to the group. But he decided to share his hope with other leaders who echoed some of his sentiments. A number of them began to talk about turning the hope into reality. They recognised that they needed to move from aspiration to serious planning in order to realise their dream.

In practice

- Be willing to share your hopes, however undeveloped they might be.

- Ask other people what some of their hopes are and explore what the common ground might be.

- View expressing hopes as something entirely different to setting objectives.

- Be open to let some hopes wither away and others gain momentum.

SHARE YOUR PERSPECTIVES

However closed off someone appears to be, there will always be a moment when they are ready to listen to the perspective of others. Be ready with your perspectives and share them when the opportunity arises.

The idea

Everybody sees the world through a different lens. We may look at the same view but each pick out different features of the landscape. Within a group there might be one orthodox perspective, but others will have equally valid ways of looking at a particular issue.

Within a group some might have a dominant perspective and assume that others will agree with their viewpoint. The most creative organisations encourage a range of perspectives so that standard orthodoxy does not weigh down innovation and debate.

John was convinced that there was only one way to organise the finance department workload. It had worked well for ten years, and surely it would work well for the next ten years. Jenny had experienced a much more flexible and adaptable work structure which was more responsive to the needs of others within the organisation. She knew that she could not force her preferences onto an unwilling boss. She needed to wait for a time when there were problems which John was less confident in handling and when he might be open to new ideas.

When the finance department was not delivering the right figures for the annual audit she illustrated to her boss some practical techniques for speeding up the process which could be used the following year.

John now readily agreed with Jennifer's suggestions and they soon became the accepted procedure. Jenny brought a perspective about what was doable from her experience in other organisations. She was initially hesitant about sharing her views but was encouraged by others to take the opportunity provided by current problems.

Once Jenny had shared her perspective and seen it implemented, her confidence grew. She felt more valued and willing to take a risk in expressing views that were contrary to the normal orthodoxy.

In practice

- Understand the perspectives of those who run the organisation and reflect on why those perspectives are important to them.

- Reflect on your perspectives and how they were formulated.

- Realise that there are always reasons why someone adopts a particular perspective. Try to understand where they are coming from.

- Remember when the perspectives you have brought were welcomed and appreciated.

- Be willing to intervene when you have a perspective which you believe is worth sharing. Choose the moment when others are receptive and want to hear about alternative approaches.

- Never be overly dogmatic about your perspectives. Present them in a way that is influential while being clear about the consequences of your preferred approach.

- Take opportunities to build on the perspectives of others rather than undermine or devalue their approaches.

- Share your perspective with some trusted others to test out how feasible it is.

53 **SHARE YOUR TIME**

YOUR TIME BELONGS to you and to your team and to the organisation paying your salary. How best do you share your time between all those who have a claim on it?

The idea

How possessive should you be of your time? Everyone wants a slice of your time, including you. Time is a precious commodity that is not to be wasted or used wantonly. How then do you ration it?

Your boss has a big stake in your time. He or she can shape your objectives and put a clear framework around the use of your time. A good boss will give you lots of flexibility about how best to use your time to deliver those objectives.

We may feel aggrieved if someone refuses to see us, or if we receive an automatic response to our e-mail saying that the recipient is not intending to read e-mails for a defined period. Just as we feel aggrieved in these circumstances, other people may feel the same when we shut them out.

Be assertive enough to set down a framework about how you want to use your time. You might want to say that time slots will only be available for half an hour or that meetings should never be longer than one hour.

One way of sharing your time is to say to your team that a number of hours a week are at their disposal and ask them how they want that time to be used to best effect.

An approach you could take with your boss is to reach an agreement about how the broad blocks of your time are to be allocated in relation to different activities and then use that as a framework to ration your time.

Matthew felt pushed in so many different directions by both his boss and his team. His first reaction was to be very possessive about his time, which tended to close him off from others. His second reaction was to talk with his boss and his staff about how best to share his time. The outcome was a broad agreement with his boss and a more realistic understanding with his staff about what elements of his time were available for which purposes.

In practice

- Might it be helpful to view your time as a shared resource between your boss, your colleagues and your team?

- Can you view your time as a precious commodity split up into half-hour, or hour-long chunks which are then allocated to particular priorities?

- Can you be even bolder in splitting up and allocating your time?

- Might you invite your staff to decide how they want to use the proportion of your time that you are happy to share with them?

- What will help you be less beleaguered about how you use your time? Can you ration the blocks of time to particular types of personal impact that are important to you?

54 SHARE YOUR FEEDBACK

QUALITY FEEDBACK HELPS inform and shape our future intentions. If we view feedback as a gift we will both welcome and want to give it.

The idea

Organisations that encourage feedback are often responsive and adaptable. Feedback from clients and customers may say as much about them as it does about us, but it always contains nuggets of truth. Feedback from our staff may hurt when we feel that our efforts are not as appreciated as we would like, or that our intentions seem to be misunderstood. But perception is reality, so if the feedback is that we need to improve in certain areas, then it is folly to ignore that advice.

In healthy organisations feedback is a two-way process. Our boss may or may not invite feedback and jumping in boldly with critical feedback may not be the best way of trying to influence them. Feedback is irrelevant if it is dismissed without proper consideration.

Before giving feedback we need to try and create an atmosphere in which feedback is invited and welcomed. A leader can be asked whether they would find feedback helpful. Provided there is a good balance between positive and development comments, most people will be happy to receive feedback if it is given in a constructive way.

Feedback that is sensitive to the context someone is in and is steering them in a particular direction can have a long-term, positive impact. If you are known as someone who gives good quality feedback, those who want to improve their contribution will seek your feedback.

Liz was hesitant about giving feedback to her boss after he had chaired a meeting that went badly wrong. She decided not to tackle this head-on, but she did want to raise the subject with her boss. In a private conversation, Liz asked her boss how he thought the meeting had gone. When she got a non-committal answer, Liz asked gently whether he might handle a future meeting in a slightly different way. Her boss admitted that the meeting had not been perfect and asked Liz for any suggestions. This gave her the opportunity to express some views. She did not have to press her case too hard as her boss clearly accepted that the next meeting needed to be conducted differently.

In practice

- Seek feedback regularly as it will always contain nuggets of gold.

- How might seeing feedback as a gift affect your attitude to the giving and receiving of feedback?

- Who is inviting you to give feedback and how do you want to use that opportunity to best effect?

- Is there someone you might want to give feedback to who might not immediately be receptive? How might you do that?

SHARE YOUR EXPERIENCE

Your experience is unique. Drawing on the width of your personal experience can provide you with more insights than you might readily acknowledge.

The idea

We often underestimate the range of experiences we bring from the different aspects of our life. We may sometimes feel uncertain about the relevance of those experiences and think that they are not transferable. For example, a parent's experience of dealing with toddlers in tantrums or teenagers in a sulk is highly relevant to dealing with difficult people at work. Organising volunteers in a club, community or faith group will have helped you develop a set of skills to motivate people that is highly relevant to many work environments.

We often think that we can only draw on our most recent experience and that experiences from five to ten years ago are irrelevant. Technology and organisational politics will have significantly progressed in the preceding five to ten years, but human nature does not change much. Experience from previous negotiations or handling financial disruption will be equally relevant. We may think that today's advanced technology means that what we learnt a few years ago is now irrelevant. Technology may mean that analysis can be done more quickly, but the need to make considered judgements about people and situations remains just as important today.

Sharing your experience is not about harping on about the past and implying that "things aren't what they used to be". But it does mean using past experience to provide insights about risks, outcomes and likely patterns of behaviour.

When sharing experience, the appropriate tone is rarely "this is how it needs to be", but is more an insight of how the next steps might unfold. It is important to leave a choice about how the experience is interpreted and not be dogmatic about your views.

Mohammed had worked as a member of the audit team in a number of different organisations. In a previous organisation the relationship between the departments was excellent because of the trust that had been built up. In his current organisation, there was a strong level of suspicion. He wanted to draw from and share his previous experience but knew he had to do it carefully.

Mohammed waited for an away day when the audit team was considering how to manage its relationships with other departments. Mohammed asked if it might be helpful if he drew from previous experience. When he got a positive response to this he was selective in identifying three particular features from the working relationships in his previous organisation. Mohammed chose his tone well and his suggestions were taken up with alacrity.

In practice

- What experience do you bring from other spheres that you can contribute?

- What, from your earlier work experience, can you draw on more fully in your current workplace?

- How might you bring your experience of what is working well into discussions about the future in your organisation?

- How do you ensure that you do not undervalue your previous experience and are confident enough to draw from it?

56 SHARE YOUR NETWORKS

ˉOUR NETWORKS ARE a valuable resource. When you introduce two people to each other and it leads to good outcomes, your role is likely to be recognised as an important contribution.

The idea

Over time we build a network of those we have worked with, with whom there is shared experience and mutual trust. Networks often revolve around the workplace or professional associations that have brought people together. The development of e-mailing, texting and social networks has made it much easier to grow and keep in touch with wider networks.

The challenge is how we use networking in a way that is both personally satisfying and professionally worthwhile. This is not about using people in a manipulative way. It is recognising that we live in a wider community and that putting people in touch with each other can be a valuable contribution.

Social networks can be a huge drain on our time. But when used in a focussed way, social networking can enrich us and enable others to find contacts who can enable them to solve problems.

Sharing your networks needs to be done with care. Friends and colleagues may not want to be introduced to other people and their desire for privacy is paramount. Sharing your networks runs the risk that others will now begin to draw on your contacts and ignore you. That is a risk worth taking if sharing your networks increases your influence with a wider range of people.

Zara kept her networks to herself and was not keen to share the names of consultants she had used before in her previous job. She felt proprietorial that the consultants were there to assist her and not other people. When specific requests came in for skills which matched those of the consultants she used, she reluctantly decided to share their contact details. The effectiveness with which these consultants contributed to the wider business won Zara a lot of credit. In retrospect, she wondered why she had hesitated to share these details for so long.

In practice

- How wide is your network? How is it growing?

- How can you use your network more to gain understanding about a wide range of issues that are important to you?

- What might be the potential consequences of sharing your network with your current colleagues?

- Can you use social networking more widely as a means of both gaining understanding of and influencing others?

SHARE YOUR HESITATIONS

WHEN WE SHARE our hesitations we are being authentic and showing that we are merely human. Enabling others to work through those hesitations with us can equip us to handle them constructively.

The idea

We all have hesitations. Even the person who looks super confident is likely to be hesitating about some of the decisions they need to make.

A hesitation is not a sign of weakness, it is an opportunity to pause and consider whether our approach is the right one and whether we need to adjust our perspective or plan. A hesitation may come from a sense of unease that we cannot fully explain: sometimes it is our subconscious telling us that something is not quite right.

Continually sharing lots of hesitations may cause others we work with to see us as being unsure and indecisive. But sharing our hesitations with those we trust helps us get valuable input about the next steps to take. When we have worked through our hesitations with these trusted others and reached a way forward, the resulting impact may well be greater because our colleagues have felt part of the process of reaching that decision.

Nathan was unsure whether to launch a particular financial appeal for the charity of which he was Chief Executive. There were lots of rational arguments in favour of this appeal, but he was unsure about whether the timing was right. He shared his hesitations with a cross-section of people, including a couple of trustees and some funders. It became a shared issue and the outcome was to delay the financial appeal until the start of the next year. He now felt much more confident about planning for this forthcoming appeal after working through his hesitations with others he trusted.

In practice

- See your hesitations as the opportunity to re-assess your way forward.

- Talk to those you trust about your hesitation and discuss alternative ways forward.

- Seek to build a shared view about the next steps to take.

- Accept that showing hesitation can sometimes build your credibility and not undermine it.

58 SHARE YOUR RANDOM IDEAS

SOMETIMES THE RANDOM ideas that come from left field can be valuable insights. Sharing these random ideas can help build a reputation for innovative thinking and can mean you are seen as a person worth listening to.

The idea

Everyone has random ideas from time to time. You could be on a walk or in the bath and the thought "what if we did it this way?" might come into your mind. You might be working through an issue and have some apparently bizarre thought about how it can be tackled. We easily dismiss random thoughts as irrelevant. But sometimes it is these slightly wacky ideas that can offer new insight and rejuvenate our thinking.

Posing the question about how a complete stranger might address a particular issue could allow us to think of very different approaches, one of which might be pertinent. Forcing ourselves to list ten ways of tackling an issue will take us beyond the two or three approaches that come to us naturally and force us to be innovative and draw from our wider experience. It is just possible that one of these unorthodox approaches could be particularly useful.

While our random thoughts might be entirely random, our brain is constantly processing information and experiences. These seemingly random thoughts could in fact stem from a mix of past experiences. While these "random" thoughts are not necessarily right, they are worth looking at instead of being dismissed.

Being creative can mean systematically following up on our ideas and looking at what is transferable from our other spheres of work or culture. The range of ideas drawn from these multiple spheres may seem random, but from these apparently random ideas can come insights that change the direction of our thinking. Building a reputation for turning random insights into constructive ideas will further enhance our influence and credibility.

Georgia had a reputation for bringing lots of ideas. Her colleagues tended to dismiss most of her ideas as impractical, but they always listened to Georgia because she often brought perspectives that were different. Her colleagues encouraged her to keep sharing her random ideas, even if most of them were not followed up on. Georgia knew she had to be careful not to deluge people with wacky ideas. She recognised that she needed to be selective about the timing of these suggestions and not to be put off if most of them were not taken forward.

In practice

- Create space in which you can have random ideas.

- Treat your random ideas seriously.

- Talk about your ideas with others if you think there might be something of value in them.

- Encourage others to share their random ideas.

- When an idea turns into a creative way forward, acknowledge and celebrate the value of that idea.

59 SHARE YOUR SKILLS

Our skills are precious assets. We may want to keep them for ourselves but being generous in sharing our skills builds genuine appreciation from others.

The idea

We each have skills in certain areas. We can often take for granted what we are good at and not fully appreciate these qualities. Some skills come naturally to us, or perhaps we have developed them over time. We can get frustrated when others do not recognise our skills or do not appreciate that their background and life experience has given them a different set of skills to the ones we have.

Having worked as a private secretary and press secretary to several UK cabinet ministers, I learnt the skill of writing quickly and succinctly. I sometimes take this skill for granted and can be frustrated if others are less adept in this aspect. Sharing this skill is sometimes about offering to do the writing while others contribute in other ways, and about passing on techniques and encouraging others to develop their approach to writing in a clear and influential way.

Recognising what you are good at and offering to use those skills to assist your boss or other colleagues is a way of being generous that benefits them without causing you too much angst. If you are skilled at negotiation, how can you help a colleague develop their negotiation skills? If you are good at handling conflict, how might you enable someone else to become more confident in dealing with them?

Sharing your skills is a very practical way of building your impact through assisting others and enabling them to develop similar skills. In this way you build a network of people who are grateful to you for the assistance you have given them. A network of allies is always useful.

Archie had a lot of experience in handling conflict situations and was always willing to discuss with colleagues how they might handle similar situations. Archie was mindful that he should not tell people what to do in a particular situation. He brought valuable insights about possible approaches based on his previous experience. Archie was appreciated by his colleagues because he was willing to share his experience and was not dogmatic in advocating one particular approach.

In practice

- Recognise the skills that you bring and do not undervalue them.

- Be willing to deploy these skills for the benefit of your colleagues.

- Be open to mentoring and enabling others to learn similar skills.

- Do not expect others to embrace your skills instantly. Recognise that skills often take a long time to develop and become established.

SHARE WHAT YOU HAVE LEARNT

SHARING YOUR LEARNING with others maximises the likely impact of that learning. If you keep your learning to yourself your contribution will be much less than you hope.

The idea

We are constantly gaining new knowledge and insights. Our first inclination might be to keep that learning for ourselves. Why should we share it with others when the information might come in useful?

If you are able to "keep your ear to the ground" so that you are alert to the ideas, preferences and approaches that are developing, you will be sought after. This is not about destructive gossiping, but about picking up understanding, distilling it and sharing it where you think it is accurate and helpful.

As a university lecturer you will have picked up information about the attitude and approach of students. Sharing that understanding with other colleagues can enable them to respond quickly if there are concerns about the way courses are put together or the expectations that are being put upon students.

There will inevitably be occasions when others use information you tell them as their own and get credit for it. But in the long run it is well worth gleaning and sharing knowledge as it builds up your reputation for being alert to what is happening and your ability to identify trends.

Hazel had an excellent network within her organisation and enjoyed catching up with a wide range of people. She knew most of what was happening at work and the senior leaders in the organisation knew that if they wanted to know the overall mood of the organisation on particular issues, Hazel would be able to give them an astute perspective. Hazel was never indiscrete and would refer to the generality of views and not quote individuals. She built up a reputation for discretion and was trusted by both junior and senior staff. Because she was willing to share her learning she became an influential member of the organisation.

In practice

- Be willing to keep learning and growing your understanding.

- Be open to share the intelligence you have gleaned in a constructive way. See sharing your learning as part of being a responsible citizen of your organisation.

- Watch out if you are too possessive of your knowledge.

- Recognise that when you share your learning you will not always get the full credit.

- Accept that sharing your learning is a powerful way of influencing others.

SECTION G
ENSURE

61 ENSURE CLARITY OF EXPECTATIONS

It is always worth ensuring that there is clarity of expectations. If there is ambiguity or uncertainty, there are bound to be dissatisfied people. Your personal impact can be maximised if expectations are clear and delivered.

The idea

If your expectations and those of your boss are different, someone is going to be unhappy. You may feel that you have delivered on your expectations while your boss is wondering why you look so happy when his expectations have not been fulfilled. Agreeing on expectations in advance reduces the leeway for ambiguity and provides clarity towards your goals.

Expectations are inevitably going to change as external factors are taken into account. But there is a big difference between your own expectations changing in your head and agreeing on those new expectations with the people you are working with.

Building clarity of expectations requires thinking ahead about what is both ambitious and reasonable, combined with effective communication with those who have an influence on those outcomes. Shared expectations can create a powerful alliance of energy and focus towards the delivery of those expectations.

If there are no expectations it is difficult to measure progress and may result in a random set of outcomes. If expectations are too rigid they can become outdated and irrelevant because they are not adaptable to changing circumstances.

When expectations are unclear, it is worth the angst and effort to clarify expectations so that you and your boss are as clear as possible about the outcomes you are seeking to deliver. When you agree on specific expectations with your boss and then deliver on those expectations, your credibility rises and your personal impact is enhanced.

Fred had been commissioned to write a report and review whether investment in beekeeping projects in an African country had been worthwhile. He wanted to be absolutely clear with the sponsors about the type of report they wanted and what areas they were seeking recommendations on. Once he had a clear brief about the people he should to talk to, the length of the report and the scope of the recommendations, he was satisfied that he could then progress. This clarity of expectations meant that he entered the project with confidence and knew that it would be a satisfying and potentially influential piece of work.

In practice

- Be clear what your personal expectations are in any activity.

- Understand where your boss is coming from in terms of their expectations.

- Agree on a set of expectations with your boss and share them with those working closely with you.

- Have an agreed way of reviewing those expectations and taking account of the changing circumstances.

- Have milestones in place to take stock of progress towards those expectations.

- Keep testing whether those expectations are both ambitious and doable.

62

ENSURE THE ENVIRONMENT IS RIGHT

ENSURING THAT THE physical environment is conducive for the type of activity you want to take forward or conversation you want to have is an essential prerequisite for success. Good environments don't just happen, they require careful planning.

The idea

You will be unlikely to ask someone to marry you in a noisy and smelly environment. You are likely to be very careful about the type of environment you let a toddler run around in – the environment needs to be safe and contained. Most of us work better in some environments than others. We may be able to work on a computer in quite a noisy environment, but may need a quieter context in which to think through issues and plan ahead.

Getting the right environment for a meeting is an essential prerequisite for success. Deciding on the seating layout can make a big difference: are people seated on the sides of a long thin table, or are they around four sides of a smaller table? Will people have eye contact with each other? With there be any problems about people hearing each other? For what types of meetings would it be better to dispense with a table and invite people to sit in a circle?

If a meeting is to be successful its participants need to feel that they are valued and can contribute. They need to be seen and able to be heard. Participants need a chairperson who is leading the process but is not too dominant in their deliberations.

When you meet someone informally, choosing the environment

can influence the flow of the conversation. If you want a thoughtful reflective conversation a quiet environment where you cannot be overheard is important. If the conversation is intended to be a lively exchange of ideas, then a more upbeat environment might help set the right tone. If it is a difficult conversation, privacy will be paramount.

Dawn wanted to build a stronger partnership with one of her colleagues. She decided that the busy office environment was not the right place to have this conversation. She invited her colleague to join her for coffee at a cafe. In this lively atmosphere the two talked about a number of different topics and agreed that the conversation had been well worthwhile. Dawn's choice of environment had worked well to build a lively sense of personal exchange.

In practice

- Observe what sort of conversations work best in different environments.

- Be deliberate in choosing the environment in which you have a conversation.

- When you are responsible for meetings, decide on the seating layout and format in advance.

- Always ensure there is good eye contact and audibility.

- Do not be inhibited from moving furniture around in order to create the right type of environment.

- Be willing to move into a different sort of environment if the one you are in is not working.

ENSURE YOU PACE CONVERSATIONS

GETTING THE PACING of a conversation right enhances the opportunity to have bigger, personal impact – if it is too slow people get bored quickly and can lose interest.

The idea

The pacing of a conversation can make a big difference to its success. Knowing how long has been allocated for a meeting is always helpful. If someone says to you that they can only give you five minutes of their time, do you get flustered or feel resentful that you are only being given such a limited period of time? Or can you zoom in on the headline points or the key question you want to ask?

We often approach conversations or meetings with a huge amount of clutter in our minds. Getting ready for any conversation or meeting involves simplifying the points we want to make or the questions we want to ask. At one extreme there is the "elevator pitch", which is what you would say to someone if you had just 30 seconds with them in an elevator. If you know what your key point is you can then pad it with key facts or perspectives if there is time.

If you know a conversation has been allocated the maximum time of 30 minutes, how do you use that time to maximum effect? The starting point is to think about what the other person or people will want out of the allocated time, so you can be responding to their needs as well as getting your points across. It can often be helpful to agree in advance how a 30-minute period is split between say, two or three topics. Brief and focussed scene-setting can help pace a conversation.

Sometimes it is helpful to say at the start of a conversation what type of interaction it is going to be. Is it about exchanging information, or working through particular problems, or looking more strategically to the future? Once participants know or have agreed on the topics and the nature of the conversation, it is much easier to then pitch the type of contribution and its pacing at the right level.

Watch what nervousness does to you. Does being nervous lead you to talk more quickly or more softly? Be mindful of the way in which you can fall into habits that may be unhelpful. Be conscious of how best you respond to your own nervousness.

Ben knew that if he was unsure what he wanted to get out of a meeting he tended to talk too much and ramble. He was thinking aloud and was therefore not consciously pacing a conversation and was unaware when others wanted to contribute. Ben learnt that he had to be deliberate about the pace he set in conversations and hold back more often to let others explore their ideas.

In practice

- Be mindful about your preferred pace in conversations.

- Recognise what happens to you under stress – does the pace of your conversations get quicker or slower?

- Be clear about what you want to contribute to conversations and be wary of using too many words.

- Always remember that conversation is two-way so be aware of talking excessively or being very quiet.

64 ENSURE YOUR INTERVENTIONS ARE TIMELY

GETTING THE TIMING right for your interventions can significantly affect your personal impact. Too soon and your comments are forgotten, too late and the conclusions have already been reached.

The idea

What matters is not just what you say, but how you say it and when you say it. A valid criticism of some groups is that participants contribute according to seniority, with the most important person speaking first. By the time the last person is invited to contribute, everything that needs to be said has been said and the contribution either becomes repetitive or non-existent, with neither outcome benefiting the personal impact of this participant.

It is useful in any group to see how people normally contribute. You may feel that you have to go with this flow, at least for a while – what matters is having something to say that is interesting, brief and relevant.

Sometimes we get into a routine where we always want to contribute early, or always want to wait until a particular person has spoken. It can help to observe the routines we are adopting and assess whether they are helpful. Deliberately varying the pattern in which you speak will mean that people take more notice of what you have to say.

You may want to come into a conversation early to help set a tone or to influence the parameters of a discussion. On other occasions you may want to contribute part-way through in order to reinforce a particular direction or steer a conversation in a different way. What matters is making deliberate choices about when you make your interventions rather than just because you "feel like it".

Sometimes you will not get your timing right: the judicious response is then to withdraw and wait for a more appropriate moment. Sometimes the moment has come and gone and it is better to leave your intervention for another occasion.

Annette had a tendency to speak early in conversations. She wanted to get her points across so she could then relax. She was disappointed that her points often seemed to be ignored. Annette decided that she needed to adopt a strategy of deliberately making contributions at varying points on different agenda items. This element of surprise meant that people were more willing to listen to her. It also meant that she was deliberately choosing the point of intervention rather than forcng herself into any particular pattern.

In practice

- Observe who makes interventions that are most influential and look at the timing of those interventions.

- Be mindful of your default pattern of making interventions.

- Deliberately vary the timing of when you make contributions and the length of those contributions.

- Do not feel you have to rush to contribute when you think your case is better served by letting a conversation run for longer.

65 ☹ ENSURE YOU LEARN FROM YOUR MISTAKES

O NE OF THE best ways in which we learn is through mistakes. Being honest about that learning can further increase your personal impact.

The idea

Our mistakes are precious as they force us to re-evaluate our approach and can lead to learning that radically improves our personal impact. If we did not make mistakes we would not learn. If we put ourselves in a situation where we are unlikely to make mistakes, our cautiousness might limit our impact.

Of course, it is right to avoid situations where you are bound to make mistakes. If you do not speak french it is dangerous to be the lead negotiator in a meeting where you need to do so. In this situation you need to have either an excellent interpreter, or someone else who does the negotiation in french, or the overall responsibility for negotiation should be allocated to someone else. There is no point in creating a situation where you are going to fail.

On the other hand, putting yourself into a situation where there will be a mix of successes and relative failures can enhance your ability to contribute.

Your openness about learning from mistakes can further enhance your credibility and therefore your potential impact. A senior leader is going to want as a project leader an individual who has both a track record of success and who is able to learn quickly from mistakes.

Louis was petrified that his advice as an economist would be wrong.

He knew that making predictions was an uncertain business. But it was his job to look ahead and set out plausible options. He recognised that the best course was to say what he thought based on his professional observations and judgement, and to recognise that some of his predictions would be right and others would not be accurate.

Louis kept learning from his observations. When he got an assessment wrong he would readily admit it. His advice was sought after by senior people in the organisation because they knew that Louis would say what his professional judgement was telling him, but would also recognise quickly when his advice was wrong and would not insist that he was right.

In practice

- Remember the mistakes you learnt the most from: how has that learning benefitted you?

- What mistakes are you having to live with? Have you fully absorbed the learning from those mistakes?

- How will you maximise your learning when things go wrong in the future?

- What type of mistakes do you not want to make again?

- What attitude of mind will you have to future failures or mistakes?

ENSURE YOU RECOGNISE THE PATTERNS

RECOGNISING THE PATTERNS of interaction or behaviour within organisations enables us to focus our contribution in a way that is likely to be at its most influential.

The idea

We all have routines. Most organisations have patterns of activity and behaviour. Recognising those patterns and working with them helps sharpen our input and impact.

An organisation's financial year or reporting cycle provides an underpinning pattern of activity. Other patterns result from the personal style and the approach of influential individuals. These patterns may evolve over time, and are likely to change radically when individual leaders move on.

Recognising patterns is helpful in terms of using energy efficiently. But rigid patterns can restrict the opportunity for creative debate and inhibit progress.

There may be some rigid patterns of behaviour that need to be addressed. Certain groups might always oppose recommendations for change because it has traditionally been their response. Recognising such a pattern can help in deciding what approaches will win people around. Recognising patterns includes understanding your own patterns about when you are at your most creative and when you are at risk of being defensive.

Recognising the behavioural patterns of the people whom we want to influence helps us understand how best to influence them. If we know that they are more receptive when in certain moods, or more receptive if they are provided with particular types of information, we can choose the way we approach them to ensure the best possible outcomes.

Eliza wanted to see if she could become more influential with her boss. She observed the pattern in her boss's working day and decided he was at his most receptive at about 5 o'clock. She deliberately dropped in on him at that time with good news to put him in a more constructive frame of mind. He was then more likely to be willing to spend time with Eliza talking through the issues she wanted to raise with him.

In practice

- Be mindful of the patterns that work best for you in focusing your time and energy.

- Observe the patterns of others and note whether the ability to influence others varies depending on the time of the day or the week.

- Keep observing your own patterns and how best you can use them so your personal impact is stronger.

- Note the behavioural and decision-making patterns in those you want to influence and decide how best to respond to them.

67 ENSURE YOU ASSESS LIKELY REACTIONS

THINKING THROUGH LIKELY reactions can help you prepare your interventions and be able to respond to the reactions of others.

The idea

When preparing for a negotiation, thinking through the likely reactions of other parties helps you develop both your content and approach. Assessing the reactions of those you are negotiating with is being mindful of their likely instant reaction and their considered reaction after a period of time. Knowing that somebody might tone down their reaction after some reflection helps us not to respond too quickly to an initial adverse reaction.

If you have a difficult and potentially unpopular message to get across, it can help to pave the way by lowering the expectations of others. If the sales figures are likely to be indifferent for a particular month, lowering expectations can mean that when the actual figures are published, people are pleased that they are not worse.

Sometimes it is not possible to gauge likely reactions. You have to push on and put forward the best case you can and not be dependent upon explicit approval.

Assessing your own likely reaction to an unexpected situation is also important so you are not thrown off course. If you know that you are likely to have a particular reaction you can prepare for it and not be thrown by the situation.

Aaron was about to present a proposal to a company's Chief

Operating Officer which involved spending to save. Aaron anticipated that there would be a degree of scepticism from the COO and prepared his presentation carefully. He noticed that the COO was particularly interested in two or three aspects, which Aaron then elaborated upon. When the COO began to look bored, Aaron knew that it was time to do the final punchline in the presentation and then move it to questions.

In practice

- Become attuned to the reactions of those you are negotiating with.

- Anticipate and prepare for the likely reactions of others.

- Do not be thrown if you get a blank reaction.

- Keep observing your own reactions, viewing them as valuable data.

- Be wary of changing a carefully prepared plan instantly just because you have been taken by surprise.

68 ENSURE YOU LIVE YOUR VALUES

YOUR VALUES ARE important to you, but what happens to them when you are under pressure? Do they become a touchstone for your decisions, or do they disappear from view?

The idea

Our values provide a framework for the way we live our lives and make decisions. They can be our biggest asset if they provide a touchstone for how we respond in different situations.

Our values are most obviously expressed in our behaviours, which will always be scrutinised. If our behaviour is inconsistent people may conclude that our values are at odds with each other. If our values include humanity, humility and hard work, living our values will sometimes mean exercising a balance between showing humanity and a hard edge. Humility may need to be combined with the hard edge of making tough decisions.

When you want to have an impact on someone, understanding their values always helps. If you are conscious of the values that underpin someone's approach to life you can assess how you best respond to those values. What is the synergy between your values and those of the people you want to influence? If there is a common set of values it is much easier to build rapport. If the values appear to be different you may need to tread more warily.

Bella put a strong focus on the values of openness and transparency in her job as a senior manager at a hospital. Each team needed up-to-date data from the other teams to do their job well. But the teams tended to be competitive and keep information private. Each team thought they were being open, but they were only sharing information at the last available opportunity. Bella had conversations with different colleagues to persuade them that greater openness and transparency would benefit the hospital as it would enable the teams to work in a more open and coordinated way. Bella's emphasis on openness and transparency was so obviously right that her persistence began to change people's behaviour and practices.

In practice

- Be explicit to yourself about the values that are most important to you in the workplace.

- Be willing to share those values as evidence of your contribution.

- Seek to understand the values of the people you wish to influence in order to build synergy and empathy.

- Recognise what happens to you when your values come under pressure.

- Recognise that being consistent in your values will help build your credibility and impact in the longer term.

ENSURE YOU KEEP COMMUNICATING

Communicate, communicate, communicate. Do not think that because you have communicated the message once it has got through and that you do not need to communicate it again.

The idea

Effective communication is a neverending process. The good communicator will have honed their message and be able to repeat it again and again and yet make it sound new on each occasion. You may become bored with the message you are communicating, but repeating it to different audiences is an important way of developing your influence and impact.

The message that becomes clearer and sharper through retelling needs to sound as if it is being given for the first time. As soon as it looks stale, its impact will diminish. One of the best ways of keeping a message alive so is to keep adding in short, up-to-date stories that illustrate the message and demonstrate its relevance.

You may want to use different words to communicate a message to the Chief Executive or receptionist. Consistency is important but the approach needs to take account of the audience and how readily they will appreciate the message.

Communicating effectively means using a range of different approaches that include written, oral and electronic means. People absorb messages through different means – some need to hear a message on a number of occasions before it is fully absorbed.

It is important to keep communicating successes. Although you are modest and do not think you need to draw attention to the successes of your team, using a range of different approaches to reinforce your team's successes is part of your responsibility as the team leader.

Always remember that communication is two-way. You may have messages you want to communicate, but beware lest you get into a dialogue of the deaf. Understanding what people are saying to you and reflecting those perspectives in the way you communicate with them is more likely to mean that they will want to engage with you.

It is important to be mindful of when you stop communicating. If work pressures are high, or if there are difficult issues to address, the absence of communication may unsettle people. Continuing to communicate, irregardless of the pressure, is necessary for any organisation to be both engaged and engaging.

David was leading an organisation through a merger with a different part of the agency. He communicated well at the start but became so involved in the detail of the next steps that he stopped communicating either in writing or in person. There was a growing sense of alarm in his organisation about whether his silence meant that there were problems. Rumours began to circulate about large scale redundancies. The truth was not nearly as drastic as the rumours. The fact that David had stopped communicating meant that the fears and worries were much greater than they need have been.

In practice

- Assess how good you are at keeping up good communication.

- Be honest about what sort of communications work best for you and use them well.

- Consider how you might widen your means of communication with your staff, colleagues and other key stakeholders.

- Ensure that communication is two-way so there is dialogue rather than you just communicating messages.

- Consider your next steps in improving communications with those you want to have the most impact upon.

ENSURE YOU CAN WITHDRAW

YOU ENJOY BEING in the fray and having an impact on others within the organisation, but you need the opportunity to be able to withdraw to rest, recharge and renew.

The idea

The leader who has impact is able to be at the centre of the action and yet able to withdraw smoothly, and subsequently return to the action. You do not have to be on the front line all the time.

It is not a sign of weakness to withdraw. Withdrawal is appropriate when it is time to renew your energy or rethink the strategy. It is time to withdraw when you have passed the baton to others who need to be given autonomy without you looking over their shoulder.

There will be times when a tactical withdrawal is necessary. You have made your pitch but the time is not right for final decisions to be made. You lose nothing by withdrawing and waiting for a more appropriate moment. It is better to withdraw quietly so wounds can heal rather than battle on and end up with more painful injuries.

If a proposal you are putting forward does not receive approval from the majority you have the choice of fighting on, or withdrawing and then seeking to influence others in favour of your perspective. When you withdraw you might also be planning to modify your ideas so they are more compatible with those held by the majority.

Sometimes you need to withdraw to let your people renew their energy. If you fight hard without giving your people the opportunity to be renewed, you may end up fighting alone.

Martha was pushing her boss to agree to an investment in a new product. She was not getting a lot of support and wanted to keep fighting. But she sensed that now was not the time to push the issue for fear of getting the "wrong" answer. Martha decided that a tactical withdrawal was the best course of action. Martha then talked to a number of different people in the organisation about the particular product she was developing and ended up with broader support. She felt confident that in six months she could return with her updated proposal and would likely receive stronger support.

In practice

- Train yourself to be alert to when you need to go forward and when you need to withdraw.

- Don't see withdrawal as a defeat. See it is a pragmatic act which preserves your strength and reshapes your perspective for another day.

- When you are very busy, always keep open the possibility of withdrawing and taking a break.

- See withdrawing as a necessary step to reshape your perspective and not as an expression of failure.

71 REMEMBER WHAT YOU ARE GOOD AT

WHEN YOU FEEL deflated or under appreciated, always remember what you are good at. Draw confidence from situations in which you can contribute well.

The idea

Our confidence levels can be fragile. We may be feeling buoyant and optimistic one week but, after a couple of setbacks, we can feel more hesitant and unsure of ourselves. When our confidence begins to dip our sureness of touch can become less secure and our effectiveness can diminish.

Remembering what you are good at can help to ensure that your confidence does not dip too much. This might mean looking at notes of appreciation you have received over the years or remembering the clients who have particularly benefited from your contribution, or the patients who recovered because of the quality of the healthcare you had ensured they received.

Our well-being depends partly on returning to the secure knowledge of what we are good at. This provides us with a firm foundation for maintaining our resolve when we feel under appreciated or subject to criticism.

If the confidence loss goes on for a period it can sap our energy and credibility. When we know we are in danger of losing confidence, we may need to put ourselves in a situation to remind ourselves of what we are good at. It might mean encouraging others to give us direct, positive messages. If we know we are appreciated by some colleagues around us, this can stop a dip in confidence from becoming too stark.

It is also about remembering what we are good at outside our work environment. The fact that we are appreciated as a good parent, friend or neighbour can reinforce our confidence levels in other spheres. Some of that confidence will rub off into our demeanour at work.

Ollie felt dejected by his boss's dismissive attitude to two recent reports that he had written. Ollie tried to keep reminding himself about the positive feedback he kept receiving from his clients. He knew that he was good at working with them. Outside of work he knew he was a good dad and a well-respected committee member at the golf club. If the boss was not going to show appreciation, Ollie could still rely on the respect that he received elsewhere as a means of keeping up his resolve and impact.

In practice

- Remember what other people say you are good at.

- Believe that their positive comments are true.

- When your confidence begins to dip hold in your mind practical examples of things you do well.

- If your confidence dips, talk to people who you know will lift your spirits.

- Write down on a piece of paper what people tell you you are good at.

72 REMEMBER LESS IS MORE

SOMETIMES THE MOST powerful interventions are brief. By speaking excessively we can blur the significance of our contribution.

The idea

We have all had the experience of listening to someone who goes on for far too long. Their words become a blur. We have forgotten what they are trying to say; we switch off.

The most influential speakers are often economical in their use of words. They use short sentences and ensure that they are appealing to both our rational and emotional needs and expectations. If a speaker has one clear point we are much more likely to remember it than a sequence of ten bullet points. Perhaps three points is the maximum we can absorb.

We may feel strongly about several different aspects of a problem. But if we articulate eight aspects that need changing it is quite likely that by the end, points one to three will have been forgotten and five to eight will have been ignored. To have maximum impact we have to be selective so that we are saying fewer, but key, points that matter rather than many points that dilute the message.

The patient will not absorb a long list of factors affecting their medical condition. The patient wants to hear simple, key facts and know the next steps they need to take to aid their recovery. The good doctor knows that if they want behaviour change from the patient, their instructions have to be simple, clear, doable and memorable.

If you want to have an impact on your colleagues, being selective about the points you want to make will increase your credibility. If you deluge them with a range of necessary improvements, they will think you are being critical of them and are not likely to respond positively. But if you can focus on two or three key points and express them in a supportive way, you are likely to have much more impact than setting out a longer list.

Harriett could not stop talking in some meetings. Whenever she opened her mouth she was ignored. When she was given tough feedback she resented these comments, but gradually realised that what mattered was not the quantity of what she said but its focus and quality. She began to discipline herself to make no more than three points, however strongly she felt about a wide range of issues. Gradually she became more influential and recognised the value of keeping her contribution tighter and not saying everything she knew about a particular topic.

In practice

- Beware if you want to make a long intervention or write a long e-mail.

- Try and crystallise your thoughts into two or three key points.

- Pride yourself on sending short rather than long e-mails.

- Use texting as a means of making short interventions.

- Observe how others use short interventions effectively.

73 REMEMBER WHY YOU ARE HERE

You are here for a reason. Someone has appointed you or you have chosen to be where you are.

The idea

You are where you are either because you chose to be there or because someone asked you to be there. You can feel stuck and annoyed about the position you are in and the past may seem irrelevant and the future very uncertain, which may mean that you are not enjoying the present.

Your current situation may not have been your original intention. You may feel aggrieved that the organisation you are now working for is losing money, as when you were appointed it was building a new market and there were high expectations of success.

Remembering why you are here is partially about accepting responsibility for the decisions you took. If you feel that you are not in a good place, what matters is believing that you can now make choices which will either move you into a different space or enable you to make your current situation more bearable.

You may be finding life to be tough as a senior administrator in a busy organisation such as a hospital. Remembering why you chose to work in healthcare can help you keep up your commitment and morale even though the current environment is difficult. Remembering why you are where you are will always help put the current issues into a wider context. Remembering the type of difference you want to make can help renew energy when you feel drained.

Edward was passionate about improving the education for children with special educational needs. He worked for a charity which was providing wider opportunities for young people with sight problems. Money was tight and the support from government seemed limited. The requests for assistance from affected families were numerous. Edward felt caught in the middle and found his energy drained and his commitment sagging. Edward's wife kept encouraging him to remember why he had joined the charity. Reminding himself of why he was there helped him keep up his resolve even in the most difficult of circumstances. He was grateful for these timely reminders from his wife.

In practice

- Remember the choices you made and the reasons that led to where you are now.

- Encourage other people to remind you why you are where you are when the going gets tough.

- Accept that not all your choices will have worked out successfully, but that all your choices were made for the best of reasons.

- Do not beat yourself up if you now feel you are in the wrong place.

- Think coolly and clinically about how you want to move on.

74 REMEMBER THAT YOU HAVE A HINTERLAND

LIFE IS NOT all about work. Our hinterland is everything else that we are interested in and engaged with that gives us energy and insight.

The idea

There is a popular saying that "all work and no play makes Jack a dull boy". We may think that the harder we work the bigger our impact, but the opposite might just be the case. If our life is dominated by work the number of other influences that inform our contributions at work will be eroded. Part of what makes us effective at work is our understanding of the wider issues in the society in which we live. Unless we are keeping up with news, talking with our neighbours and sharing ideas with friends, we will not be fully equipped to be an effective contributor at work.

Our hinterland gives us an important perspective on current trends, current fashions and ways of thinking alongside changing norms and expectations.

We may want to keep our personal hinterland completely separate from our work so that our work environment does not intrude into our personal well-being. But drawing clear boundaries does not mean that our work and personal lives are entirely self-contained. There will be good practices and ideas that we glean from our work environment that are relevant to the way we organise our daily lives or contribute in the community in which we live. There will also be insights from the society and community in which we live that are relevant to the contributions we seek to make in the work context.

The difficult task is getting the balance right so that experience from our hinterland informs the way we contribute at work, while at the same time ensuring that the pressures of work do not affect our spheres of family and community.

Naomi thoroughly enjoyed her family and leading a brownie pack. She understood the pressures on parents and the way children learnt and was good at balancing discipline with a scope for creativity. Naomi was also a graphic designer who was conscious of the need in her day job to balance discipline and creativity. She was good at encouraging the staff who worked with her to develop disciplined techniques alongside innovative approaches. Naomi's experience of leading a Brownie pack and bringing up her children reinforced the importance of encouraging her junior staff to be disciplined and structured, while always looking for creative and new ways of doing things.

In practice

- Be clear what aspects of your hinterland are most important to you and essential to your well-being.

- Keep drawing lessons from the experience of your hinterland that are relevant to the current work you are doing.

- Be mindful when your hinterland begins to get too crowded.

REMEMBER THAT LIFE IS NOT A DRESS REHEARSAL

75

LIFE IS FOR real. We only get one opportunity at life, although we are continually learning from our different experiences.

The idea

There can be a risk that we see life as a bit of a game in which we can continually experiment with possibilities. We may be exploring which of our skills we can apply best in the work environment. Continued experimentation is important, but there is a point when we need to focus and decide what we are going to do next.

Effective preparation is important. A practice interview can be very valuable in preparing us for the type of questions we are likely to be asked at the interview. The dress rehearsal is an essential part of preparing ourselves, but only if it helps us to approach the main performance with a quiet confidence and a flexibility to respond to pressure.

Working in an organisation means that we are on show all the time. We are having an impact whether we like it or not. In this sense there is no dress rehearsal because we are being continually assessed by our peers and our staff. Every contribution we make is for real. In the work environment we are always learning and always developing our performance and contribution. As we keep refining what we do and say, our impact grows.

Life at work is not like a play which has a clear plot, set lines and a known outcome. The drama of work continues to change. There will always be unexpected scene changes and characters will move on and off the stage in unpredictable ways. We will be continually evolving our part in the drama of our work.

Elliott enjoyed taking part in amateur dramatics and excelled at taking a role and making it his own. He loved the scenes where he made the audience laugh. His role at work seemed very different – he was acting a part, but as soon as he had learnt his lines the plot changed. He drew from his experience of amateur dramatics in being clear-headed and in coordinating his tone of voice and his actions. But playing the part of a senior manager was more demanding as he needed to keep changing his lines to fit the evolving context. One consistent theme between his two worlds was the need to make people smile.

In practice

- See work as a drama in which you are a key player.

- Remember that you are always being watched and every performance is affecting the way you are viewed.

- Enjoy the way the scenes keep changing.

- Remember your lines but be willing to adapt them to suit the evolving situation.

- See life as a continuous mystery play rather than as a dress rehearsal.

76 REMEMBER YOUR FAMILY HERITAGE

We are more influenced by our heritage than we often realise. Understanding our family heritage enables us to realise more fully how we impact others.

The idea

When I understand someone's family heritage and, in particular, the characteristics of the individual's parents, many of the reasons for the individual's behaviour become clear. We are our parent's children whether we like it or not. Their characteristics flow through us mentally, physically and emotionally.

Whatever your father or mother was good at, there is a reasonable prospect that you will have qualities in that area as well. If your father was thoughtful but indecisive you may share some similar characteristics. If your mother was disciplined and courageous, it is quite likely that you will also possess those attributes.

Sometimes our family heritage creates artificial limitations on our expectations. Because your father never rose above a certain level of seniority you may assume that you will not go above the same ceiling. This respect for a parent can create a self-limiting belief that going above a certain level is either impolite to the memory of a parent or likely to be impossible.

Sometimes our parents will have been good at personal impact in a different context to the one we are in. Reflecting on the applicability of their skills to our situation can give us fresh insights into gifts that we have not fully drawn upon. If your father was a miner perhaps there are qualities of toughness and resilience that have been passed onto you that you have not yet fully utilised. If your mother was a teacher, perhaps there are gifts of teaching and stretching the thinking of others which you have inherited but not yet fully developed.

Kate was grateful for the care and attention from her parents. She had inherited her father's drive and single-mindedness. From her mother came her strong sense of curiosity. She enjoyed applying these attributes in her approach to her work, but the fact that her parents had never risen to positions of seniority inhibited her. Kate kept reminding herself that her parents believed in her and would be delighted if her career was more 'successful' than theirs had been.

In practice

- Celebrate the attributes from your parents that you most appreciate.

- Believe that you are quite likely to be good at what your parents excelled in.

- Think through what could be attributes from your parents that have not yet blossomed in you. How can you embrace these attributes more fully?

- Reflect on the extent to which the respect for your parents might limit your self-belief about what you can do.

- Remind yourself that your parents would be delighted to see you influence others well in your work.

77 REMEMBER THOSE WHO LOVE AND SUPPORT YOU

In a busy working life it is easy to take for granted those who love and support you. Remembering their needs and supporting them in their endeavours is crucial for your own well-being and your long-term impact.

The idea

We are very dependent upon those who love and support us. Without their commitment we would flounder. Our personal impact is dependent upon our emotional well-being. Those who love and support us have a profound effect on that sense of well-being.

We may feel that we have invested hugely in important relationships. When we are pressured at work we keep drawing from the reserves built up in those relationships. There is a risk that we might begin to drain those reserves beyond their limits. Keeping a network of close friends may be central to retaining your equilibrium. We need to be able to talk to loyal friends who have supported us over many years, but we can easily take their support for granted and fail to renew bonds of love, affection and support.

Those whom we love or are in companionship with help keep the blood of life flowing through us. If we want to keep fresh we have to keep nurturing these bonds of love, without which life would be so much duller.

Callum had the drive to work hard but after six months of intense pressure at the bank he began to feel listless. He had relied on the love and support of his wife and perhaps taken her for granted. She was there to support him when he was feeling exhausted. Callum realised how dependent he was on his wife for support and admitted that he had taken her love and support for granted. They reached a new commitment with each other about the support she gave and what he would do in return. He was confident that this healthy new contracting would both strengthen his marriage and help him keep a better equilibrium at work, enabling him to influence others without looking too intense or drawn.

In practice

- Treasure those who love and support you and acknowledge their importance to you.

- Recognise the significance of the love and support you receive from others and its effectiveness in helping you keep your equilibrium.

- Acknowledge how much of your influence and impact is dependent on those who love you providing you with emotional support.

78 REMEMBER WHAT LIFE IS FOR

CONSTANTLY REMEMBERING WHAT is important in your life provides you with a rationale for the way you use your energy and enables you to cope with the vagaries of life.

The idea

Remembering what is important in your life provides the rationale for handling tough situations and having the personal impact that you think is necessary. If you believe that the activity of the charity you work with is particularly important and that you have a strong sense of vocation to be part of that work, then this personal belief can carry you through the most difficult of situations.

If you are in the fortunate position of having a strong sense of vocation or calling, this personal resolve can enable you to handle situations of conflict with an inner confidence. If you believe that you are making a positive difference in the work you do, this can give you a passion to keep going and the willingness to push boundaries even when you are met with setbacks.

You may feel a sense of calling to be a teacher, social worker, probation officer or priest. This sense of calling provides an inner resolve to make a difference, but can cause you to keep banging your head against a brick wall when you need to be more flexible and adaptable. A sense of calling can sometimes make us blinkered, which means our impact may not be quite as subtle as it might need to be.

There are moments when it is right to reconsider what is important to you. What is driving you in your 20s may not be what is providing our motivation in your 40s. You might want to re-evaluate in your early 50s what has been the richness of your experience and how ou might want to translate that into a different set of priorities oing forward. Perhaps you are at a time of life when your priorities witch from doing to enabling others to do things well.

Sofia thought that life was all about creating a home for herself and her family. Once she had done this she rethought her priorities and decided that there must be more to life than creating a home, however important that is. She decided she wanted to teach and delighted in the progress of the six-year-olds with whom she was working. Sofia felt her life was much more fulfilled with the combination of both teaching the children and the creation of her own home.

In practice

- Do you feel any sense of vocation or calling in your work?

- How clearly can you articulate what is important in your life?

- In what ways do you need to evolve what is important in your life to take into account new circumstances?

- To what extent do you feel dissatisfied with your answer to the question of what is important to you in life?

- What practical steps might you take to widen your view of what is important in life so that you can influence a wider range of people in new ways?

79 REMEMBER WHAT LIFTS YOUR SPIRITS

KNOWING WHAT LIFTS our spirits and makes us feel that our efforts are worthwhile is important to our continued well-being and impact.

The idea

When do we tell ourselves that something was worth it? When we work hard and get no immediate return it is our perseverance and resilience that carries us through. When we see results from our efforts, our spirits can be lifted. When I work as an executive coach with leaders and see them tackling problems in a way they had not thought possible before, it lifts my spirits. I know my efforts are not wasted and I can end the session encouraged and even elated.

What lifts your spirits may be the satisfaction of a piece of work well done, positive feedback from clients, a higher output figure than expected or staff survey results that show that your area of work is appreciated. It is worth asking ourselves regularly what lifts our spirits and how we ensure we enjoy and internalise that positive feeling.

For some this will be a quiet inner satisfaction. For others there will be an expression of joy. What is important is that you understand what lifts your spirits and then ensure that you put yourself in situations where that is going to happen. This is not about selfish indulgence: it is about preservation and keeping up your own resolve and well-being in order to sustain the right level of impact.

If you are in a busy period at work you may need to think carefully about what will lift your spirits at a busy time. It might be having coffee with people who cheer you up, or remembering to have a talk with your mentor because you always feel good about yourself after such conversations.

Andrew was conscious that what lifted his spirits during a busy day was a conversation on the telephone with his toddler son at lunchtime, three cups of coffee during the day and brief conversations with one or two colleagues whose voices and laughter would always cheer him up. He knew that if he did not put himself into a situation where his spirits were lifted he could feel flat and exhausted by the middle of the afternoon. He tried to include these crucial ingredients no matter how busy he was.

In practice

- Be honest about what lifts your spirits and what dampens them.

- Put yourself in situations where your spirits will be lifted.

- Recognise what type of brief activities will lift your spirits during a busy day.

- Make time to talk briefly with colleagues whom you are encouraged by.

- Talk briefly to family members when you know they will lift your spirits.

- Enjoy the moment when your spirits are lifted and do not go back into work mode too quickly.

REMEMBER YOU ARE HUMAN

OUR HUMANITY IS our strength and our weakness. Our humanity has given us intellect and emotions. It has also given us vulnerability and the ability to experience pain and pleasure in equal measure.

The idea

We are not robots driven by a computer programme. We are not predictable and certainly not always rational. We are not machines doing what other people tell us to do.

Our humanity means that we bring emotional warmth alongside rational thinking. We can be clear one minute and distracted the next. We can be enthusiastic for one project and within a week have become bored with it. We can be a delight to live with, and yet morbid and morose a few hours later.

Our humanity also means that we are unpredictable. We may set off on a particular course and end up in a very different place. Sometimes we will do all the right things in terms of influencing other people. On other occasions, we can be acting in a haphazard and uncontrolled way.

Sometimes we can be fearful of our own unpredictability and variable confidence. Our imperfections mean that we will not always get it right. We need the support of friends and the forgiveness of many. Thankfully, everyone else is human too, so we need to be able to accept each others' unpredictabilities and be forgiving of inconsistencies.

Hollie was uneasy because she did not maintain the standards that were important to her in the quality of her work and her relationships. She gradually accepted that she was human and that there was no way she was going to be perfect. Hollie accepted her imperfections and inconsistencies and that her humanity was one of her greatest strengths and not a liability. This made Hollie much more relaxed about herself and in her dealings with other people. This meant she became more influential and had much more impact than she had ever expected.

In practice

- What aspects of your humanity do you find it most difficult to accept?

- How has your vulnerability in certain situations given you a sensitivity about how best to handle these situations?

- What aspect of your humanity which you have previously tried to hide do you want to acknowledge?

- How can you accept that the unique blend of characteristics in you is both special and distinctive? You are a unique person who has a tremendous amount to contribute – "warts and all".

81 CREATE YOUR FAN CLUB

BUILDING A GROUP of people who will support you and be a fan club for you will help widen your influence as they will be your advocates across the organisation.

The idea

It can be hugely valuable to build a network of supporters. Most of this is a spin-off benefit from your contribution to the organisation. If people see that you are adding value their natural inclination will be to want to support you and be associated with you.

A good leader creates followers as a result of both the quality of what they do and the way they do it. The more visible you are and the more you can generate human exchange and warmth, the greater the likelihood that you will grow your fan club. If people inside and outside of your organisation view you as approachable and clear-headed, they are more likely to identify with you and support your ideas.

The more you acknowledge the contribution and support of others the more likely they are to support you. It is worth trying to build supporters in unlikely places. If the receptionist at your office thinks well of you, they can become one of your most vocal advocates. Your fan club will grow significantly if you treat each person, irrespective of their role or grade, in a similar way, acknowledging the value and distinctiveness of their contribution.

Remember that fans can be fickle. Fashions change – people who support you one month may be supporting someone else the following month. Sit lightly to your measure of how much support you have. What is important is that you are consistent in building the quality of a range of relationships.

Oscar was a popular manager at the call centre. He was always encouraging and cheerful and gave time to others in order to help them become more confident in dealing with difficult customers. Because of his success and popularity he was promoted. His successor was equally effective: he now became the favourite of the staff working in the call centre. Oscar was regarded as less accessible as a result of his promotion. While Oscar was disappointed that his fan club had become smaller, he recognised that he needed to take a more background role so that his successor could be centre stage.

In practice

- Be conscious that you are building supporters or critics all the time.

- Show appreciation on a regular basis for what people have done for you.

- Be visible as often as you can and show that you are interested in people.

- Demonstrate that you are willing to make tough decisions for the good of the organisation.

- Do not expect that your followers will cheer you on overtly.

CREATE TIME FOR REFLECTION

Creating space for reflection is essential to help maintain your equilibrium and perspective. Space for reflection is not an optional extra.

The idea

There is a risk that we may regard constant action as virtuous and time for reflection as an optional extra. But if life is all about activity we may wear ourselves out or end up going round in circles.

We need to create space to reflect on which aspects of our personal impact have worked well and those that have worked less well. We need to do an honest stocktake about where we got it wrong and what we learnt from that.

Space for reflection puts the various pressures on us into perspective. Unless we take a step back we are not able to think through our priorities and who we want to influence. Good reflection enhances our personal impact and does not detract from it. Sometimes it is important just to spending time thinking without rushing.

Personal reflection allows us to sit outside ourself and observe our actions and behaviours in an objective way. It gives us the opportunity to think through how we might handle situations in the future so that our personal impact can become more targeted and effective. Good personal reflection time is rarely wasted. If we find ourselves falling asleep then perhaps we are over tired and need to switch off mentally and physically anyway.

We need to be deliberate in creating time and space for reflection. It might be short spells of quietness during a busy day. It might be an hour at the end of a week noting down what went well, what our learning has been and what we want to experiment with going forward. It might be a half-day every six months to reflect with a coach or a trusted colleague and identify important themes about our actions and attitudes.

Lola was frenetically busy as an IT consultant. She was at the beck and call of a lot of people who valued her expertise. Lola knew she needed to take a step back and be clearer about the type of work she wanted to do. She needed to structure her life and work in a more proactive way and not just rely on being responsive to others. She set aside time to work through her priorities with a coach and ended up with a much clearer prospectus for the forthcoming year. The time for reflection had shaped her attitudes and approach in a way which gave her more confidence and enjoyment going forward.

In practice

- Insist on having time for reflection.

- Create shafts of stillness during a working day when you can breathe and take stock of things.

- Decide what pattern of reflection works best for you and develop a weekly, monthly and annual cycle.

- Be conscious about who you reflect with best.

- Use an experienced coach to help you crystallise your learning and plan effectively for the future.

CREATE YOUR REPUTATION

WE ALL HAVE a reputation. The challenge is to create the reputation you want with the right people in the right timeframe.

The idea

The people around you will each have a reputation for something. Some will have a positive reputation based on previous contributions. Others might have a negative reputation because of what they have done or not done in the past or because of their attitude. Just like them, you too will have a reputation.

Reputations come and go quickly. You are only as good as your last victory. Achieving a positive outcome in a difficult situation wins respect and builds a positive reputation. But if you are seen to lose out in the next negotiation your reputation can decline rapidly,

The best of reputations take a long time to build up and ideally are based on both respect and affection. People will watch to see how you handle disappointment or critical comments. If you display an emotional reaction, your reputation may be weakened. If you demonstrate resilience and determination to learn and move on, your reputation can be further enhanced.

Reputation is linked to respect. One of the most disastrous ways in which reputation can be damaged is when someone "loses it" and shows an aggressive or emotive reaction. When someone is seen to lose control a positive reputation can be quickly tarnished.

Once a positive reputation has been built up, it is important to avoid indiscretions that will destroy that reputation. The collective memory about successes may be fairly short-term, but that of inappropriate behaviour or reactions is long-term and can be terminal.

Blake wanted to build up his personal reputation at influencing key people. He built up key relationships with people and worked hard to have interesting and valuable things to say. His reputation grew stronger. On one occasion he lost his cool and was angry with a colleague. News of Blake's harsh words passed around the department quickly and this indiscretion tarnished his reputation. It took a long time for others to be willing to be fully open with him again. He worked hard at rebuilding his reputation and made certain that he did not make the same mistake again.

In practice

- What type of reputation do you currently have?

- What type of reputation would you like to have in the future?

- Who do you want to invest in so that your reputation is enhanced?

- What are the risks of you doing something that could markedly damage your reputation?

- How might you avoid a situation where your reputation could be adversely affected?

CREATE YOUR OWN TEAM

You CANNOT ACHIEVE everything by yourself. Creating your own team is an essential step to ensure that what you want to achieve is successful and has the impact you want.

The idea

In a good team each participant works effectively with other colleagues. There is a strong sense of mutual collaboration and working towards the same ends. There is a complementarity of skills and experience.

Your personal impact depends not just on your personal contribution but on the efforts and impact of the people around you. You may inherit a team but it still needs to become your team.

Creating your own team starts from clarity about the impact that you want your team to have. Consider what type of qualities you are looking for in your team members, and what type of ways of working and attitudes are most likely to lead to the desired outcomes.

Spending time creating and building your team is rarely wasted. Time spent on recruitment is fundamental to success. You will want to delegate to your team and ensure that their impact is consistent with the direction you are setting. Time spent steering and mentoring your team is always going to be an important priority.

A leader needs to generate a sense of ambition and a clarity of thought in their team, alongside an ability to bring out the best in each other that is more than "the sum of the parts".

Annabel was a team leader at an insurance company. She had been asked to take on additional work, which meant that they had to combine two teams. Annabel was clear that she wanted to create a coherent new enterprise which would have a constructive impact across the whole organisation. She took the team away for half a day and used a team coach to help them work through both their priorities and their behaviours.

Annabel set the tone for the away day but invited all the participants to share their perspective of how they were going to work together effectively. She built a shared view about relative priorities going forward. Annabel's personal impact would now be magnified because the whole team was acting in a united way. They had a shared agenda, an agreed way of working together and pooled their resources and relative capabilities.

In practice

- Do you need to be clearer about the capabilities of your team and the impact you want your team to have?

- What mix of skills are needed to deliver that impact?

- How best do you work with existing team members to ensure that together you are able to deliver the impact you desire?

- How best do you bring in new team members to ensure that the combined effect of the new and existing members creates significant impact both inside and outside the organisation?

CREATE YOUR LEGACY

Having a specific goal about the legacy you want to create gives valuable focus to help ensure your personal impact is directed clearly.

The idea

Your legacy may be tangible or intangible. The legacy for an architect is the building they have designed. The legacy for a road engineer is the motorway they helped construct. The legacy for a teacher will be mature adults in twenty years time. The legacy for a probation officer might be that fewer crimes have been committed.

What do you want your legacy to be? This question can give focus to the contributions you want to make. A desire to create a legacy gives an impetus to the type of personal impact you want to have and brings clarity in looking at the opportunities available to you and how best to use them. You may be faced with uncertainties about the future and barriers to progress. But the more you can identify opportunities for forward momentum, the greater the likelihood that you can create irreversible progress.

You may feel that resources are tight and that constructive change is not possible, but often when resources are restricted there can be an opportunity to question existing ways of doing things and advocate and then implement change that uses resources to better effect.

It can be worth looking at the jobs you have held before to identify what has been the legacy of your efforts. This review can provide you with examples that help you build your momentum for the future.

The most powerful legacies are often about people. Your approach and the values you bring can be passed on to a subsequent generation.

As a former Director and then Director General in the UK government, there are a sequence of policies that I was responsible for that benefited a range of people. But what gives me particular pleasure is meeting individuals who worked with me ten or twenty years ago who talk about what they learnt when we worked together.

Laurence worked for a police force and thoroughly enjoyed the camaraderie with his colleagues. He was based in a city where crime rates were high and wanted his legacy to be a reduction in crime rates amongst young people. He was committed to make his contribution through both enforcement and through preventative measures. He got to know a cross-section of young people and presented a human but firm face of the police force. He worked tirelessly and was reassured to see a gradual reduction in the crime rate. This was exactly the legacy he had hoped to contribute to.

In practice

- What type of legacy do you want to leave?

- How does that type of legacy influence the sort of personal impact you want to have?

- What proportion of your legacy do you want to be about events or about people?

- What are your next steps towards building your legacy?

86 ⊙ CREATE HOPE FOR THE FUTURE

Creating hope for the future is about building shared aspirations that lead to a greater momentum than would otherwise have been the case.

The idea

The more you can stimulate constructive conversation about the future, the better. Whatever the current issues might be, if there can be quality consideration about what the future might hold, this reflection can build hopes for the future and provide a "pull" factor to keep motivation high.

If hopes for the future are just an irrelevant dream, they are not likely to have much impact. But if those hopes are based on reality, they can have an aura of credibility and become a reasonable aspiration.

A picture about what the future will hold can provide a framework for the way you use your energy over forthcoming months. Dreaming about the future and then sifting through those dreams to differentiate between the absurd and the dream worth aiming for can provide you with fresh motivation.

Every Olympic athlete has hopes for the future that start as a dream and become more realistic as training takes shape. The hope of a future Olympic medal provides an incentive for the individual and the team to focus their efforts on and to see how far they can go. There is no guarantee that a future hope will become a reality. But if you believe that hopes can come true and if you prepare and train effectively, then your hopes might just turn into a 'gold' medal.

You may aspire to have an impact on a particular policy, operation or individual. Defining and then holding on to that hope, and doing all the preparation and training that is needed, can lead to delivering the impact you want. Unless you have an aspiration about making an impact you will never get anywhere near it.

Mary wanted to work in the French office of the business. With this firm hope for the future she decided to build her case by enhancing her language skills, doing some projects jointly with the French operation and building her networks in France. Her aspiration led to a clear strategy which helped build up her credibility to work in France. Mary needed to persuade the French country director that she should be appointed. She let her interest be known and gradually built her credentials so that she became an obvious choice to take the next available role in Paris.

In practice

- Turn your dreams into practical hopes.

- See your hopes as both aspirational and doable.

- Prepare a careful plan which will enable you to take practical steps towards fulfilling that hope.

- Work hard to deliver the hope but do not hold on to it too tightly because the preparation might be leading you to other outcomes that you might not have been aware of.

CREATE SOURCES OF ENERGY

ENERGY IS NOT finite. We need to create it and renew it in both ourselves and our colleagues.

The idea

We create physical energy through many different ways. We have learnt to harness the use of water and wind as well as burning fossil fuels. The way energy is generated in various places will depend on what resources are available and how best they can be utilised.

The energy in you and your team will come from different sources. Individual energy might come from personal drive and motivation, the encouragement from others, the response to progress and the delivery of effective outcomes. Energy within a team might come from progress made to-date, the stimulus of working together and the hopes of what is achievable.

We each have a personal responsibility to be conscious of our energy sources and to nurture and not exhaust them. As a member of a team we have a corporate responsibility to be mindful of what gives a team energy and what grows and saps that energy.

Sometimes what makes the critical difference in terms of personal impact is whether you have more energy than others. Who is going to give up first is a pertinent factor. When Olympic athletes are running towards the finishing line the one who keeps their energy up the longest crosses the finishing line first. Sometimes our view might prevail when everyone else has given up.

Being utterly relentless can undermine our position if we annoy and aggravate people. But if we are able to keep up our energy and continually adapt our approach, we can end up having the impact and influence we want.

Creating sources of energy is about being systematic in nurturing our physical, mental, emotional and spiritual well-being. Can we do more of whatever gives us energy? If we keep our energy levels topped up the impact we can have may be more than what we had ever thought possible.

Aidan knew that to keep his energy high he needed a combination of the right diet, fresh air at lunchtime, the support of two or three key friends and good quality sleep. He knew he had to maintain this balance and keep looking for new sources of energy. He had recently taken to going for long walks with his son during the weekend which helped him to nourish his energy levels. He knew he had to keep assessing his energy levels and be mindful if they began to sag.

In practice

- Keep monitoring your energy levels and observe what raises or lowers them.

- Keep building new ways of guarding and nourishing your energy levels.

- Observe the relationship between your energy levels and those of your team.

- Be conscious about how you can contribute to raising team energy levels.

- Accept that you have the prime responsibility for preserving and enhancing your energy levels.

CREATE NEW WAYS OF LOOKING AT ISSUES

ENCOURAGING NEW WAYS of looking at issues can provide new insights that can turn a problem into an opportunity.

The idea

Each of us has tried and tested ways of addressing tasks. We know what works for us and want to keep using approaches that have been successful before. But perhaps there is more than one way to tackle a problem.

We may believe that the right way to influence others is to use approaches that have always worked well in the past. Perhaps we have become too predictable and therefore not as effective as we would want. It is rarely possible to generate new ways of looking at issues purely with a blank sheet of paper. We need the stimulus that comes from observing others and picking up a range of ideas. Visiting a similar type of organisation or a different department in our own organisation can introduce us to new approaches to tackling similar issues.

We can also draw from how issues are tackled on the sports field or in international diplomacy or community politics. If we are constantly open to learning something new and picking up new ideas, we are likely to be accumulating a range of ideas and perspectives that will come in useful.

To help widen the range of possibilities in your mind, you could ask yourself how a famous politician or diplomat or sports coach might handle a particular issue. Thinking about their approach can help provide new creative ways of looking at issues.

Generating a variety of ways of looking at issues helps us to broaden our approach to personal impact. You are then less likely to be predictable and therefore will be taken more seriously.

Mario was leading a waste management team in a busy city. He was using tried and tested techniques, but he was conscious that approaches to recycling were changing quickly. He recognised that he needed to keep up to date with practices adopted elsewhere and set aside time to visit other cities. He was impressed by the innovative approach some of them were using and returned with a set of creative ideas. This wider understanding gave him the ammunition to persuade his bosses to invest more in waste management in order to save money over the longer term.

In practice

- Prioritise learning how other people are tackling similar issues.

- Do not dismiss innovative approaches without properly considering them.

- Visit other teams or situations to see what you can draw from their experience.

- Pride yourself on spotting and developing creative ideas.

- Remember that being too predictable is unlikely to help your cause.

CREATE A SOFT LANDING

CREATING A SOFT landing is about how you prepare and react to not achieving the success you want, so that your confidence is enhanced and not damaged.

The idea

What happens if we fail at something? Do we go into deep despondency and dejection? Do we become grumpy and difficult to live with? Do we set so much pressure on winning a particular argument that if we fail to do so, we feel our approach is undermined and our confidence sapped?

The high-jumper who clips the bar falls onto a padded base, gets up unharmed and is ready to attempt that height again. The knowledge that they will have a soft landing helps with the motivation to try again. We need to create the equivalent of the soft landing so that when we seek to overcome high barriers we know that we will not be hurt if we are unsuccessful.

When we try something and do not succeed our first inclination is often to criticise ourselves followed by possibly criticising others. We will have a list of excuses and reasons that can waste our emotional energy and sap our confidence.

Preparing for a soft landing is about recognising that you "win some and lose some" and that there will inevitably be some adverse emotional reactions that you have to live with. The type of support you receive from friends and trusted colleagues when you do not succeed is important. The high-jumper gets up from the soft landing and is back for another jump. We need to create conditions for a soft landing so we can get up and be ready for the next challenge.

Arthur was applying for promotion and had worked hard in preparation for the interview. He was determined to do well in the interview and thought that he could succeed in the role. Part of his preparation was recognising that he was in a job where he was learning a lot. If he was unsuccessful in his bid for a promotion, staying in his current role would be a perfectly reasonable soft landing. That gave him the comfort not to be too anxious in preparing for the interview. Knowing he had a soft landing did not reduce his motivation but did help him keep his equilibrium.

In practice

- What does preparing for a soft landing mean to you?

- Do you constantly beat yourself up if you do not succeed? How can you guard against that?

- What is needed for a soft landing if things do not go as you hope?

- How best do you balance the motivation to do well and succeed while recognising that sometimes you will not be successful?

- How helpful is it for you to remember that even the most successful teams do not win every match?

90 CREATE CREATIVITY

THE MORE YOU can create together with others the less the pressure is on you. Creating together often results in more sustainable development than if you had done it alone.

The idea

Working with others can generate a range of ideas because of differing experience and perspectives. Joint creativity can be fun when the emotional dynamics are right but can also be hard work if there are markedly different perspectives and preferences.

Attempts to work together with others can sometimes fail and resentments can build up about the reasons for this failure. It can be worthwhile for the group to take a step back and examine what has gone wrong and how they are can work more effectively together in the future. On other occasions working together is never going to work and, as with a failed marriage, the best outcome is an amicable divorce.

Creating well together requires mutual understanding about the ground rules and about how best people are creative together. Basic parameters about how meetings are convened, who summarises the conclusions, and how best discussion is stimulated can help create the right conditions for success. It is worth recognising the patterns of what makes joint creativity possible. It might be about the right physical environment, the right time of the week, and enough affirmation between the different parties about what enables joint creativity to work effectively.

When you have difficult negotiations to handle who do you work best with? Who can complement your approach and with whom can you be creative in working through solutions? Taking the initiative and saying to someone, "I enjoy working creatively with you" will often produce the positive response you want.

Loretta was a fashion designer who relished opportunities to talk with other designers. In one sense they were in competition with each other, but Loretta knew that the stimulus she got from discussing ideas with others enhanced her creativity. Loretta had to keep being innovative and yet not appear outrageous. She talked with others in the industry so she understood the trends. Other fashion designers loved talking with her because of her positive and engaging approach.

In practice

- Who are you at your most creative with and can you take that partnership further?

- What are the conditions necessary for you to be creative when working with others?

- To whom might you explicitly say you want to do more joint creative thinking?

- How best do you set aside time so that there is opportunity to work together with those who enable you to be more creative?

- How might working together with others in a creative way enhance your influence and personal impact?

91 KNOW YOUR PRIORITIES

Know your priorities provides a framework and a stability that helps provide a resilience to cope with inevitable buffeting.

The idea

The building remains standing because the walls are built on firm foundations. The cross-country route works well because there are markers at regular intervals and there is no risk of getting lost. The long walk you have planned is a success because you set the target of reaching particular points by certain times.

Some of your most successful moments might be when you are working within a clear framework with defined milestones and detailed priorities. Having a set of priorities enables us to use our time and energy in a focussed and effective way. Reaching those milestones gives us satisfaction about making decent progress.

Knowing your priorities may not be straightforward. You will be dependent upon the priorities of others, where reaching shared views about priorities is important to stimulate progress. It is not always possible to be precise about priorities because of changing circumstances. Your top priority now might be overtaken by another more important one in three months' time. But knowing there is a potential risk does not undermine the value of building clarity about priorities in order to provide a sound framework.

As you reflect on the personal impact you want to have with key people it is worth being clear about the outcomes that are most important to you. Having set out what you want to achieve it can be a helpful technique to number them in order of priority, or to note a proportion of time that you are prepared to devote to each priority, or to mark them on a scale of zero to ten in terms of their importance.

You may have your own agenda about priorities, but building agreed priorities with others is more likely to lead to the success you want. These will inevitably require a degree of compromise, so being clear what your top priorities are is important.

However important your priorities are to you, it is vital to review them on a regular basis. The wider context and your own personal views might change and the priorities might need to be altered. It is helpful if they do not need to change too frequently, or you can lose your focus and direction.

Finlay was a solicitor who had built up a successful practice and was much in demand. He knew he had to prioritise the type of cases that he was most effective in handling. Finlay wanted to lead on every case but knew that this was not in either his professional or personal interest. As he prioritised more effectively he became increasingly effective in the advice he gave. His impact grew because he prioritised his focus.

In practice

- Be willing to prioritise and keep prioritising.
- Be objective in the way you prioritise so you use your talents and time to best effect.
- Be wary about modifying those priorities for short-term emotional reasons.
- Be robust about your priorities and be willing to review them on a periodic basis.
- Seek to build shared priorities with others where possible.

92 KNOW YOUR PLAN 'B'

Having a clear plan is important but having a Plan 'B' provides important reassurance. You might also need to be prepared if neither Plan 'A' or Plan 'B' work.

The idea

The parent with a young child rapidly learns that they need a Plan 'A' if the baby is awake and a Plan 'B' if the baby is asleep. The parent also has to be ready for situations in which they can do neither because the baby is unsettled and is not willing to cooperate.

The learning that the parent gets from bringing up a young child is pertinent in the context of work. After setting priorities there needs to be a plan to deliver those priorities. It is likely to be expedient to have both a Plan 'A' and Plan 'B' in case the former is less feasible than we had hoped.

The value of having a Plan 'B' is both that you have an alternative and that you continue to have an openness in your mind that there is more than one way of delivering this priority. Having a Plan 'B' is not an admission of failure before you begin, it is a recognition that there are a range of different ways in which issues can be tackled and that adaptability is important to ensure success.

Sometimes neither Plan 'A' nor Plan 'B' works and, like the parent with the crying baby, we can feel moments of helplessness or exhaustion. The right perspective then might be to go for Plan 'C' or to bide your time until 'the baby is calmer' and Plan 'A' or Plan 'B' become possible again.

Planning the timing of your interventions is crucial for personal impact. Sometimes it is right to go for Plan 'A' now but on other occasions you need to wait until people are ready to listen and respond positively to it. When you judge the moment to be right, drive Plan 'A' forward with energy.

Gabriella was managing the rosters for aircraft crew. There was a danger of fog which could disrupt the flight arrangements. She knew that she needed to have a Plan 'A' for if there was no fog and a Plan 'B' if fog affected the airport at Jersey. She had carefully forewarned different people so they were ready for what they might be asked to do.

There turned out to be no fog but one of the aircraft had a technical problem and was taken out of service. So Gabriella needed a Plan 'C' to respond to this unexpected problem. Gabriella felt she had done the right thing by having both a Plan 'A' and a Plan 'B' in place. She responded quickly to the need for Plan 'C' and knew that she was contributing to limiting the number of unhappy customers. Gabriella got a lot of personal satisfaction from the ability to create and adapt different plans.

In practice

- Is it reasonable in most situations to have a Plan 'B'?

- How do you best balance the merits of Plan 'A' and Plan 'B'?

- How can you keep adaptable so that you would happily do Plan 'C' if that was necessary?

- How best do you keep your equilibrium so that if neither Plan 'A' nor Plan 'B' proves possible, you are still able to think constructively about the next possible steps?

KNOW THE STRENGTH OF YOUR POSITION

BEING CONFIDENT ABOUT and knowing the strength of your position is important. We need to be mindful that we can easily feel that our position is not as strong as it is.

The idea

In the heat of the moment we can have reservations about whether our evidence is robust and whether our arguments are convincing. We can become more hesitant than is necessary. When we have done our homework and prepared carefully we can be confident that what we are advocating is worthwhile, but when we are pressurised some of our reasons may feel less convincing. Being preoccupied with the doubts of others can also weaken our resolve to reach a particular outcome.

Our position is often stronger than we might think. We may have some doubts, but others will observe what we have done before and where we have been successful. We will have a reputation in the eyes of others, who will have decided how much they believe what we say and how willing they are to be convinced by our arguments.

The runner leading the race who is not confident of their position and believes they are likely to be overtaken will probably be overtaken. If the runner believes that they have the strength to continue in the position they are more likely to find the inner strength to be able to do so. Success comes from knowing the strength of your position and believing in it.

Asking trusted others how strong your position is provides a valuable cross-check. But do not accept their view at face value – ask them why they take the perspective they do. What is most useful to you are their reasons why and not necessarily their overall conclusion. At the end of the day it is your self belief in the strength of your position that matters, not the views of those around you.

Josh was negotiating with the finance department for more resources. He felt his position was strong because he could demonstrate that deploying these resources would mean more income for the company. He was initially met with scepticism from the finance department but knew that the Chief Executive wanted to see an initiative in this area. Josh was persistent and relied on the strength of his position. Eventually he got the agreement he wanted. What had kept him going was knowing his evidence base was strong and that there was likely to be support from the Chief Executive.

In practice

- Build the best possible evidence base you can.

- Be objective about the strength of your position.

- Consider carefully what is the strength of other people's position.

- Watch your emotional reactions so that a sense of criticism does not lead you to devalue the strength of your position.

- Seek objective views from others about the relative strength of your position, but then rely on your own judgement and not on that of other people.

KNOW YOUR NEGOTIATING PARAMETERS

IN ADDITION TO knowing the relative strength of your position, you need to know your negotiating parameters and agree on them with key people.

The idea

When you go into any negotiation, knowing your fixed points and the areas where there is scope for flexibility is important. Being in agreement about the fixed points with your boss and key colleagues reduces the scope for misunderstanding. Ambiguity about these fixed points in a negotiation can lead to confusion and a less-than-optimum result in terms of both outcome and reputation.

Sometimes people may not wish to agree on fixed points because they want to see the strength of the other party's case. Individuals may not want to reveal their bottom line for fear that they will be pushed to it too quickly. The good negotiator has to find out what are the considerations that matter most to those involved, while not pushing too hard on what are the absolute fixed points.

Knowing your negotiating parameters requires a sensitivity about the relationship between what matters to you in negotiations and your own emotions. Is there a risk that your emotions might either make you more rigid or more flexible than you should be? While it is important in negotiations to use your emotions to both understand where other people are coming from and to influence the way you put your points across, it is also vital to ensure that they do not destabilise your own rationale or bias your judgement in a way which you might later regret.

Ranking the possible outcomes so you are clear about the degree of acceptability of different outcomes can help clarify what aspects of your position are the most important and where you might be more flexible.

When Sarah was heading a pay negotiation she was clear that the headline increase figure must not be above 2%. She had agreed on some parameters for her negotiations but had the flexibility to decide on how the increase was split by grade and whether there might be a bonus element. Sarah gauged opinions on these variables with a cross-section of people before entering the negotiations. She reached an outcome which satisfied the negotiators on both sides that was consistent with the overall headline figure of 2%.

In practice

- In any negotiation be clear about your fixed points and why they are important to people.

- Be clear about your scope for negotiation and the parameters within which an outcome needs to lie.

- Build a picture of what matters most to the different groups.

- Be mindful that you stay objective as far as possible and be wary about your emotions taking you in particular directions.

- Enjoy working through the negotiation and be mindful that you do not create unnecessary enemies along the way.

95 KNOW WHO YOUR ALLIES ARE

KNOWING WHO YOUR allies are can affect how you influence others and reinforce the relative strength of your position.

The idea

Who are your allies at work? Having your boss and your staff as your allies is a crucial starting point. But how strong is the support from them? Knowing whether your boss is fully committed to what you are advocating or purely paying lip service is a necessary piece of information. Your staff say they are in support of what you want to do but how deep is that commitment? Are they expressing words of support because you are their boss, or is there both a rational and emotional commitment to what you are seeking to achieve?

Sometimes you can have allies in unexpected places. Someone in the finance department may have built a respect for what you are trying to do. A member of the senior team might have observed your approach to tackling difficult issues and be willing to back you.

But just as you might have allies with influence in unexpected places, there might also be unexpected critics. When you disagree with someone and they feel they have come off worse there can be an emotional scar that stays with them and influences their attitude to you and any future proposals. It is worth being mindful that there will inevitably be some people who are less than fully committed to your success. What matters is keeping these critics to a minimum and then trying to neutralise their impact.

Nurturing your allies is important so that they feel recognised and appreciated. You never know when you might need their support again so always remember to acknowledge their contribution and say thank you.

Austen thought it unlikely he could build a joint initiative involving the local authority, a government department and the police force, but he wanted to give it a try. He drew on past contacts with people in each organisation to build common cause and to create some allies. Each organisation had its own particular interest but he thought it would be possible to create a sense of shared partnership.

Austen briefed some local politicians and the local minister of parliament who became his ally in persuading others to support this joint project. The fact that Austen had built up allies in the finance department and amongst the local politicians meant that agreement was reached far more quickly than he had expected.

In practice

- Commit time to building allies.

- Accept that people will either support or ignore you for a range of different reasons.

- Recognise that you will have allies and critics across the wider organisation.

- Reflect on how you will build up your allies and neutralise your critics.

- Be willing to spend time with people building them up as allies.

- Accept that someone may be an ally on one point and a critic on another.

96 KNOW WHERE THE PITFALLS ARE

Being prepared for pitfalls, be they seen or unforeseen, helps us keep our equilibrium and keep focussed on the impact we want to have.

The idea

We may think we have a wonderful plan and thought through every possibility but there will always be pitfalls along the way. We can anticipate many of the risks and plan in advance, although we may lose our focus on the key task if we are too focussed on planning for every possible risk.

Some pitfalls are difficult to predict. The boss leaves and we lose his sponsorship, or there is a financial crisis in the business and all discretionary expenditure is halted, or there is a major dispute between two key players in the organisation which causes a lot of activities to grind to a halt.

Certain pitfalls are external and beyond our control, but some of the most acute pitfalls are within ourselves. If we begin to lose confidence, our sureness of touch can rapidly slip away. If we become overly tired our ability to be decisive in difficult situations may be undermined.

A potential pitfall is the desire to be liked. If we think that there is a sense of disapproval from either our bosses or people we are working with, we can rapidly begin to feel that we are not appreciated and thereby become more reluctant to express a view. Alternatively, our reaction to not being appreciated might be to react too assertively and believe that we can turn issues round by force of argument. We might end up with an aggressive response that undermines much of the goodwill we have built up.

Anne was the vicar of a church with a growing membership. She delighted in the variety of people who came to the church. There were plans for the development of various activities within the church, but she had not anticipated the loss of revenue when some families moved away or the criticism that arose from a group whose strong preference had been for a male incumbent.

The biggest pitfall Anne had to face was her own dip in confidence when she realised that not all the congregation was fully supportive of her. She decided to build a relationship with those who were her critics rather than ignore them. This was difficult at first but gradually her confidence grew again and her former critics were willing to accept her leadership and stopped creating rumours of discontent.

In practice

- Remember that there will always be pitfalls. Plan for those you can foresee and do not be too surprised by those that just appear.

- Remember how you have overcome pitfalls before and dealt with them successfully.

- Recognise the pitfalls in yourself which come through apprehension or a loss of confidence.

- Be amused rather than surprised when unexpected pitfalls occur.

KNOW HOW YOU RECOVER FROM SETBACKS

THERE WILL ALWAYS be setbacks and times when we need to consider changing direction. Our character and courage grows out of how we handle setbacks.

The idea

You might spend a long time planning to set up your own business, but when you look at the figures in the cold light of day you recognise that the business plan does not stack up. Initially you do not believe the figures so you do the detailed work again. If the business plan continues not to look feasible you may feel devastated that your dream is not going to materialise.

Your second reaction might be one of thankfulness that you have discovered the likely outcome before you have invested in the business. Accepting that a planned new venture is not going to be viable can either be a devastating blow or a valuable, liberating experience. You now know what course of action not to take and are now free to think about other alternatives, uncluttered by that particular dream of setting up your own business.

When you suffer a setback the key questions are, what did I learn from that experience and how best do I move on? If we see setbacks as part of life's rich experience, we can continue to learn from them and grow in understanding and wisdom.

Some setbacks will have a profound effect on our lives. When we lose our job we might not be able to meet certain financial commitments.

If we lose a crucial negotiation, our credibility within an organisation may be spent.

Perhaps we recover best from setbacks by taking a break, crystallising our learning and then moving onto the next project with renewed discipline and determination. The Olympic rower who does not win a medal needs to take a good break and then return refreshed and determined to do all the training necessary to become a future medal contender. Accepting the pattern in ourselves about how we respond to setbacks is part of the secret of recovering from them well.

It was a big blow to Patrick when he was not promoted. He had worked hard and expected to be successful. Patrick took his disappointment stoically and asked for considered feedback. He used this feedback as a basis for working with a coach about his personal impact. He recognised that he did not always come over convincingly and that he needed to build a stronger evidence base and think through some of the issues more thoroughly. The setback had been a blow to him but the consequence was he was much better prepared for any future interviews.

In practice

- Consider how you have recovered from setbacks in the past.

- Observe how other people recover from setbacks and consider what aspects of their approach you might embody.

- Look at setbacks in a detached way so that your learning is as sharp and clear as it possibly can be.

- When setbacks are severe be ready to recalibrate the personal impact you want to have so it is realistic.

98 KNOW WHEN TO STAND FIRM

THERE ARE TIMES when you are clear that you are not going to shift your position. Knowing that there are points when you will stand firm gives you a confidence to be yourself and express your views.

The idea

Sometimes we are pushed further than we are willing to go. We could be asked to say something that we do not think is true. We know we need to stand firm. We make a stand that we are not prepared to say something that is untrue. We know we are taking a risk in terms of our reputation, but often our frankness is respected and we are not expected to go further than what we believe is right.

We may want to seek the support of someone so they speak up on our behalf. When they say to you that they will support you in this area if you support them in another, you may think that the trade is reasonable. On other occasions you may say that you will consider carefully the points made by your colleague, but cannot guarantee that you will support them unless you are convinced by the merits of their case.

As an economist you may have offered advice about the merits of a particular type of investment. You see the potential advantages but are also conscious of the risks and cannot give an unequivocal recommendation. You are being pressed by people in the organisation to modify your view and give the project strong support. You know that your professional integrity requires you to stand firm. You are willing to enter a few caveats about your view which are perfectly reasonable qualifications, but remain firm that your professional view stands and that you are not going to be brow-beaten into submission.

Standing firm is never easy. You have to be clear why you are taking such a stand and be able to articulate the rationale convincingly. You may think that standing firm will endanger your personal impact. But if your reasons are cogent and are put across in a fair and balanced way, then your reputation is likely to grow rather than diminish.

Esme was an economist in an economic ministry. Her ministers wanted to adopt a particular finance approach. She was asked for her advice and carefully set out pros and cons but was clear that in economic terms the proposal was flawed. The ministers' special adviser tried to persuade her to change her mind but she decided that her professional integrity meant that she needed to stand firm. Eventually the ministers' initial enthusiasm waned and the policy was not announced. Esme was glad she had been consistent and not allowed herself to be persuaded against her better judgement to back a proposal which she did not think was economically justifiable.

In practice

- Be clear what your professional integrity is telling you when you are in controversial situations.

- Be prepared to stand firm when you believe that it is necessary.

- Prepare others for the fact that you are likely to have to stand firm so they are not surprised or offended by your action.

- Always set out your reasons for standing firm in a clear and cogent way.

- Accept that standing firm might lead to short-term criticism, although in the longer term it can often reinforce your credibility.

KNOW YOUR LIMITATIONS

BEING CLEAR ABOUT your limitations helps you avoid situations where you are less likely to be successful or, at the very least, to enter those situations prepared and forearmed.

The idea

The footballer with a stronger right foot has to recognise their limitations. The relative strength of the two feet will influence the position which they fill and the way they play. The tennis player who is right-handed holds the racquet with their stronger hand. If they held it with their left hand they would not be as successful. Accepting and living with our limitations is part of life. The footballer develops the strength of their weaker foot so that they are not caught off guard by the other team. The tennis player does not try to hold the racquet with their weaker hand.

If we know that we are not adept at giving presentations to large groups of people we either have to develop the skills to do so competently, or decide that we are never going to give that sort of presentation. If our numerical skills are not strong we may decide that we need to develop them to the point where we can hold our own in discussions involving figures, while recognising that we are not likely to be applying for a job where numeracy is of paramount importance.

Being able to live with our limitations is important. We may be able to develop our less strong points to some extent. But accepting that we do have limitations and being at peace with them is important if we are going to keep balanced and sane.

Harvey recognised that he was not good at making instant decisions. He always needed time to weigh up the evidence and to test his approach with other colleagues. He knew that he would not excel in a role where quick decisions were important. He knew he could make quality decisions on complex issues but recognised that he needed more time than others. He found his niche working within an insurance company on some of the most complicated of claims where accuracy was more important than speed. He made a massive contribution in this area. Both he and the firm recognised his strengths and did not force him into roles where his limitations came to the fore.

In practice

- Accept and do not fight your limitations.

- Try to make some progress in the areas where you have limitations but accept that you will not be perfect.

- Work in a complementary way with others so your limitations are not exposed.

- See your limitations as contributing to the humility that is part of living responsibly.

100 KNOW YOUR END GOAL

Knowing your end goal keeps you focussed on what is most important to you. Your end goal might change at different points of your life.

The idea

Prior to an Olympic Games the goal for all the athletes is to participate. For some the end goal is to win a medal, for others the end goal is to reach a final, or to achieve a personal best. The end goal is an aspiration that enables the athletes to focus their training and be fully committed to do the best they can.

Your end goal might be to become the best possible accountant or architect or supermarket manager or entrepreneur or social worker. Your end goal might be winning cases, setting up a new business, transforming the lives of young people or creating a new design that is widely acclaimed.

Our end goal might be to have the biggest possible impact on a wide range of people or we might want to focus our impact on a smaller number of influential people. Perhaps the biggest impact we want to have is on our family to enable them to have financial security and the space to enjoy life and grow.

If our end goal is about creating a better environment or better opportunities for other people, we are more likely to have a deep sense of satisfaction than if our end goal is about our own financial wealth. We have one life opportunity to have the type of impact that is important to us, enabling people to have faith in themselves and others, improving the lot of others and creating bonds of love and respect. If our end goal is to make life a better place for others, may that pervade all we do with our personal impact based on faith, hope and love, and not on personal gain.

Karen worked in a bank but was dissatisfied with the focus on financial transactions. She did not want her life to be focussed on making money. Karen switched into teaching much to the surprise of her friends. Her end goal was to have an impact on children as they learnt so that they would become responsible citizens. She respected the importance of banks because wealth has to be created if education is to be available, but Karen wanted her contribution to be directly related to the learning of young people. That was where she had a passion to make an impact.

In practice

- Be conscious of the end goals that are important to you.

- Be open to your end goals evolving over time.

- Keep a careful eye on the equilibrium between your work and personal end goals.

- Seek a coherence in your end goals that covers the various aspects of your life that are important to you.

BOOKS BY DR PETER SHAW

Mirroring Jesus as Leader. Cambridge: Grove, 2004.

Conversation Matters: How to Engage Effectively with One Another. London: Continuum, 2005.

The Four Vs of Leadership: Vision, Values, Value-added, and Vitality. Chichester: Capstone, 2006.

Finding YourFuture: The Second Time Around. London: Darton, Longman and Todd, 2006.

Business Coaching: Achieving Practical Results Through Effective Engagement. Chichester: Capstone, 2007 (co-authored with Robin Linnecar).

Making Difficult Decisions: How to be Decisive and Get the Business Done. Chichester: Capstone, 2008.

Deciding Well: A Christian Perspective on Making Decisions as a Leader. Vancouver: Regent College Publishing, 2009.

Raise Your Game: How to Succeed at Work. Chichester: Capstone, 2009.

Effective Christian Leaders in the Global Workplace. Colorado Springs: Authentic/Paternoster, 2010.

Defining Moments: Navigating Through Business and Organisational Life. Basingstoke: Palgrave/Macmillan, 2010.

The Reflective Leader: Standing Still to Move Forward. Norwich: Canterbury Press, 2011 (Co-authored with Alan Smith).

Thriving in Your Work: How to be Motivated and Do Well in Challenging Times. London: Marshall Cavendish, 2011.

Getting the Balance Right: Leading and Managing Well.
London: Marshall Cavendish, 2012.

Leading in Demanding Times. Cambridge: Grove, 2013
(Co-authored with Graham Shaw).

The Emerging Leader: Stepping Up in Leadership.
Norwich: Canterbury Press, 2013 (Co-authored with Colin Shaw).

100 Great Personal Impact Ideas. London: Marshall Cavendish, 2013.

FORTHCOMING BOOKS

Celebrating Your Senses. London: SPCK, 2013.

Sustaining Leadership. Norwich: Canterbury Press, 2014.

100 Great Coaching Ideas. London: Marshall Cavendish, 2014.

Effective Leadership Teams: A Christian perspective. London: Darton,
Longman and Todd, 2015 (co-authored with Judy Hirst).

ABOUT THE AUTHOR

Dr Peter Shaw works with individuals, teams and groups to help them grow their strengths and tackle demanding issues confidently. His objective is to help individuals clarify the vision of who they want to be, the values that are driving them, the added value they want to bring and their sources of vitality.

His work on how leaders step up successfully into demanding leadership roles and sustain that success was recognised with the award of a Doctorate by Publication from Chester University in 2011.

Peter's clients enjoy frank, challenging conversations that lead to fresh thinking and new insights. It is the dynamic nature of the conversations that provide a stimulus for creative reflection and new action. He is often working with Chief Executives and Board members taking on new roles and leading major organisational change.

Peter has worked with Chief Executives and senior leaders in a range of different sectors and countries. He has led workshops on themes such as "Riding the Rapids", "Seizing the Future", "Thriving in your Work" and "Building Resilience", across five continents.

Peter has held a wide range of Board posts covering finance, personnel, policy, communications and delivery. He worked in five UK Government departments (Treasury, Education, Employment, Environment and Transport). He delivered major national changes such as radically different pay arrangements for teachers, a huge expansion in nursery education and employment initiatives which helped bring unemployment below a million.

He led the work on the merger of the UK Government Departments of Education and Employment. As Finance Director he managed a £40bn budget and introduced radical changes in funding and accountability arrangements. In three Director General posts he led strategic development and implementation in major policy areas.

Peter has written a sequence of influential leadership books. He is a Visiting Professor of Leadership Development at Newcastle University Business School and a Visiting Professor at the University of Chester Business Faculty. He has worked with senior staff at Brighton University and postgraduate students at Warwick University Business School and at Regent College in Vancouver. He was awarded a CB by the Queen in 2000 for his contribution to public service.

Peter is a Reader (licensed lay minister) in the Anglian church and has worked with senior church leaders in the UK and North America. His inspiration comes from long distance walks: he has completed eleven long distances walks in the UK, including the St Cuthbert's Way, the South Downs Way, the Yorkshire Wolds Way, Cheshire Sandstone Trail and the Great Glen Way.